NETWORK TO
INCREASE YOUR NET WORTH

Compiled by
TONI COLEMAN-BROWN

NETWORK TO **INCREASE YOUR NET WORTH**

Published by Marketing for Coach, Ltd
Second Floor
6th London Street
W2 1HR London

www.coachingandsuccess.com
info@coachingandsuccess.com

ISBN: 978-0-9575561-1-9

Published in UK, Europe, US, Canada and Australia

Book cover and Inside Layout:
Karine St-Onge
www.shinyrocketdesign.com

TABLE OF CONTENTS

A HEARTFELT THANK YOU

It takes an incredible amount of courage to expose yourself to the world through writing. I am so proud of each and every author who has made this book possible. They each had the courage to say "yes" to this project and then the fortitude to see it through to the very end. Bravo! I want each of you to know that I consider you all to be my sister friends. We are now forever connected because of this project. I also want to say thank you for being so transparent and down to earth while sharing your gifts and expert advice. I have learned so much from each of you, and I would be remiss if I didn't call each of you by name. So thank you to Julia Shaw, Greta Douglas, Alice Heiman, Jayne Rios, Kendra Gainey, Wendi Caplan-Caroll, Cee Cee Caldwell-Miller, Kimberly McCarter, Valerie C. Wells, Kioshana LaCount, RoseMarie Couture DeSaro, Mindy Barnett, Jeselle Eli, Chikeola Karimou, Rhonda L. Moore, Kristi Ballard, Audrey Woodley, Tanesha Williams, Dr. Genevieve Kumapley, Marsha Graham, Audrey Reed, Cathryn Clarkson Finley, Cathleen Williams, Taylor Stephens, Shannoya Fellows, Lucrece Augusma, Darlene Aiken, Rogernelle Griffin, and Polly Hadfield. All together we represent 30 powerful women entrepreneurs who are making it happen BIG and using networking as our most valuable tool to increase our bottom lines.

I also wanted to take some time out to thank all of the women who agreed to become Regional Directors with the Network for Women in Business. These women have agreed to launch chapters all across the country. Not only are you all great leaders, but you are also all experts in your own right. This book is for each of you. I know that you will definitely have success as you teach others how to network to increase their net worth! And special thanks to all of our Platinum Members of the Network for Women in Business. You ladies definitely rock!

This year I asked God to align me with the right people. I've been looking for those people who have a big heart just like I do, and God has delivered. There are a few people I want to thank personally. One is Julia Shaw. We go way back, my friend. I am so thankful for your continued support and friendship. We all need someone like you in our lives—you know, those who believe in us when we sometimes don't even believe in ourselves.

I also want to give a special thanks to Greta Douglas. You are just a sweet, sweet spirit, and I am so thankful to have you on the team, helping out in any way you can. I feel like God has truly sent an angel to help on this special mission. I am just so glad that the angel is you.

I also have to thank Christine Marmoy of Coaching & Success. You have created two mind-blowing experiences for me in less than a year. Only you could do that. Keep doing what you're doing because you're helping make dreams come true, and for that you will always be blessed.

Last but not least, thank you to my family: Sandy, Taylor, and Sasha. If not for the three of you, I don't know where I would be. Thanks for driving me crazy and allowing me to drive you crazy in return.

INTRODUCTION

Someone once told me that you make plans, and God laughs. The truth of the matter is that, if someone had told me two years ago that I would be in this space right here, right now, I would not have believed them. When I first launched the Network for Women in Business, my intentions were to create, build, and grow an online network for women business owners. I wanted to create a space where they could network with each other both online and offline. I wanted them to be able to make powerful connections that could turn into awesome partnerships and joint ventures. Yet what has happened in the past year and a half has been nothing short of amazing.

The Network has grown beyond my wildest imagination. When I initially started emailing our newsletter to subscribers, we were emailing about 50 women; today we email more than 2,000 and we have almost 15,000 Facebook fans. Our members are from all over the world, and I am honored to be able to connect with so many like-minded female business owners who all have dreams and goals to grow their businesses to 6- and 7-figure businesses. This is not only exciting for me, but also gratifying.

I have often been told by many experts to ask myself what I would do even if I weren't getting paid for it. My answer is quite frankly that I would be doing exactly what I am doing right now. I am doing what I was born to do. Not too many people can say that. I am a natural-born networker who came by this gift honestly. You see, my father was the exact same way. I can remember as a little girl walking in the mall with my dad; he would stop and seemingly talk to everybody that we ran into. I can remember distinctly one day asking, "Daddy, how do you know that man?" He responded by saying, "Girl, I don't know that man. He just came up to me and started talking." When he said that to me, I was stunned and amazed. My father did not meet a stranger. Everywhere he went, he made fast friends. I'm proud to say that I'm just like him, and I believe that if he were living today as a woman and not a man, he would be doing exactly what I am doing.

I must admit that this has been a great year for me as it relates to networking and connecting. I would need three more sets of hands and feet to count all of the people who have reached out to me for some sort of "collaboration" or "partnership." Some of these proposals have been good deals, but some of them have been downright wrong for me and my business model. Therefore, one of the biggest lessons I've learned to date has been to learn how to say "NO!" Unfortunately, I've had to learn this the hard way. So to say that I've gotten burned a couple of times this year would be an understatement. Yet I've also learned that this is a part of life and we have to live and learn. I've also discovered something interesting about the process and the cycle. When I look back over the days, I realize that I've never had to dwell on a problem or an issue for very long because, as soon as something not so good happens, something amazing comes right after it. This cycle of ups and downs never allowed me the time or energy to pine over the bad things because so many good things were waiting right around the corner.

So as you embark on this journey of learning how to Network to Increase Your Net Worth from some of the most auspicious women that I've ever met, I thought I'd start you off with some nuggets of my own. These have been some of the most important lessons that I've learned as it relates to networking and building relationships. I know they will help you because they've definitely helped me. So here goes...

1. Protect Your Network

Everyone has a network of people, regardless of how big or small. Make sure you protect them. Don't allow people to market directly to your network or tribe. The people in your network are with you because of YOU! You're the person they like and trust. The best thing to do when people come to you wanting to gain access to your people is to make the introduction and then let the tribe decide on their own if they want to go further with the new person.

2. Make people earn your SEAL of APPROVAL

Remember this: A 'prospect' is just a 'suspect' until they show themselves APPROVED. Although the majority of people whom I've met are sharp and really have their acts together, a lot of people over the years have been really shady. I hate to say this, but I am just being honest. They've not kept their word, and then when you try to reach out to them, they suddenly go missing in action. So before you go all in with people you don't know, make sure to have your own litmus test to take them through to prove that they're worthy of doing business with you.

3. People will let you down. SO WHAT? GET OVER IT!

Because networking is about relationship building, it can be likened to any other type of relationship and, to be honest, in relationships people sometimes get let down. Just like people get hurt in romantic relationships, people can get hurt in business relationships. It happens. When it does, make sure you don't shut down and give up. Dust yourself off and keep it moving—and always have a backup plan.

Here's a true story:

Recently I was getting ready to host our annual Small Business Boot Camp for Women in New York City and someone I had just met offered to do my make-up for me in exchange for a vendor table at the event. I said, "Great! Let's do it!" So, she did a consultation over the phone and asked me what type of look was I going for and the whole nine yards. I was so excited that I would have a professional come out and "hook me up." Luckily, on the day of the event, something told me to pack up all of my own make-up just in case she didn't show up. So what do you think happened? Of course, she didn't show up! Hey—at least she called around 1:00 pm and said that she had gotten sick with a bad stomach virus. I'm not mad at her because I realize that these things happen, but these are the types of precautions and preparations that you might have to take when you're doing business with people you don't know.

4. Be a Person Who Keeps Your Word

When building relationships with people, they will either teach you what to do or what NOT to do. My advice to anyone who is reaching out to others seeking to build solid relationships is to try to be a person of your word. Keep your promises and honor your relationships. But when people let you down, get over it—FAST. Don't let it fester inside because, when you do, you run the risk of becoming bitter and never wanting to go out and network or do business with others again. All business transactions involve life lessons. When people let you down, make sure to learn the lesson; don't keep coming back for more punishment. And please make sure that you're not the person constantly doing all of the letting down. Make sure that your word is your bond.

5. Be a LIFTER!

Have a positive mental attitude and be a LIFTER! Be the type of person that people want to be around. Remember that we are like elevators: We are either going to take people up or pull people down, but you never leave them the same. Are you an UPPER or a DOWNER? Don't be a Linus from Charlie Brown or an Eeyore from Winnie the Pooh. Instead, be a Pollyanna who always looks on the bright side. Remember: People might not remember your name, but they will always remember how you made them feel.

Listen, I could probably go on and on with nuggets of information that I have learned since forming the Network for Women in Business, but I'm going to stop here because I know that you're anxious to hear from the sharp women in this book. What I just gave you here is a small taste of what's to come. I never knew there was so much to learn about networking, but these women blew me away with their stories, secrets, and expertise. They get it, and in this book they share it. From online to offline networking, they reveal their secrets to you. So I'd like for you to engage with the co-authors of this book on a personal level and learn exactly how they have used their networks and networking to increase not just their bottom lines, but in some cases, their minds, bodies, and souls. Take the plunge and dive in, one chapter at a time, one co-author at a time, and ENJOY!

RHONDA MOORE

Rhonda L. Moore, a health and wellness coach, is the Owner of RLMoore Fitness Consulting and Training LLC in Odenton, MD. A passionate public speaker, Rhonda's message is "Unleash YOUR Inner Champion."™ She is also a veteran of the US Navy and a breast cancer survivor.

She can be reached on

Facebook: RLMoore Fitness,

Twitter: @RLMooreFitness,

or via her website at www.rlmoorefitness.com

CHAPTER 1

NETWORKING: YOU ARE NOT ALONE

by Rhonda Moore

*A friendship founded on business is better than a
business founded on friendship.*
–John D. Rockefeller

I didn't want to go. Here it was, the night of the event, and I was looking in the mirror trying to find ways out of attending *You don't have what it takes, Rhonda. These are amazing, successful women. What do you have to offer them?*

The event was a private fitness-networking event in New York City. I had decided in January 2012—nine months before the event—that I wanted to go, but my fears and insecurities kept me from even applying until right before the deadline at the end of June. The only reason I applied was because I was sure I was going to be rejected. Surprise, surprise—they accepted me! And believe it or not, this acceptance gave me three more months to stress out about the event.

Don't get me wrong. I'm no wallflower. I was a Senior Enlisted Leader in the military. I am a breast cancer survivor. I am physically and emotionally strong. But there was something about attending this networking event that scared me.

After retiring from the military, I'd gotten into a rut. I wanted to run my own business, but instead found myself waking up every day, working out, going to my job, coming home, and doing it again the next day. This little voice in my heart kept saying, "Your passion is speaking about health and wellness. You can't inspire other people unless you get out of this comfort zone of fear. You can't do it alone."

So, here I was, three months later, walking in the door to this event. My heart was pounding, my palms were sweating. You know what I found when I walked into that room? A sisterhood! I discovered a warm group of women who all faced the same challenges and fears as me. I was only alone because I thought I was alone.

From that one event, I met my web designer and my social media specialist. Here I had been struggling to do these things myself when there was no need to. With the help of these women, my clientele is growing; I have a fabulous website, and am no longer a slave to social media.

So what was my problem? Why was I, an accomplished leader and survivor, so afraid to attend a simple networking event?

The truth is, I am an introvert, and like many introverts I can seem very outgoing and confident. But deep inside, I'd really rather be alone.

In her book *Networking for People Who Hate Networking*, Devora Zack says that if you're an introvert like me, you don't have to hate networking. In fact, she says that introverts have certain qualities that allow us to become excellent networkers.

She further explains that introverts can learn to enjoy networking by employing what she calls the "3 P's": pausing, processing, and pacing. Introverts tend to *pause* before they speak. This helps them make the most out of the networking event. Introverts also tend to *process*—or "go deep." In other words, she says that when introverts attend a conference, their inclination is not to introduce themselves to everyone there because they would rather make one or two deep connections. Finally, Zack explains that introverts tend to *pace* themselves. They know that, in order to re-energize, they need solitude, which for some might mean skipping the dinner meeting so that they can be fresh for the morning networking breakfast.

Reading this book helped me to understand that I am a good networker because I am an introvert. The main reason for this is because of my natural ability to focus the attention on other people when I network. This makes me more attuned to the needs and communication styles of the people around me. I will ask more questions and probe more deeply, which tends to cause people to really like me because I show a genuine interest in them!

So, the next time you are feeling fearful of attending a networking event, remember the Golden Rule of Networking: Treat people how they want to be treated. Focus more on what you can GIVE them than what you can GET from them.

When you intentionally build relationships with others whom you can help, the Law of Reciprocity kicks in and they want to help YOU too. In order to get to the next level of success, you have to move from independence to interdependence. The way to do that is through building strong relationships with others.

So how can you avoid the pain I felt when I first started networking? Let me share with you what I like to call my top ten do's and don'ts of networking.

THE TOP 10 DO'S AND DON'TS OF NETWORKING

The Top Five Things NOT to do:

1. **Not knowing what your goals are**
   Why are you networking in the first place? If you're only doing it because you think you should or because "everyone" tells you that you need to, you're going to waste your time. Have a clear goal for your networking activities. Are you looking to get leads? Build referrals? Find new people to collaborate with? Generate sales?

2. **Not having a plan for what you're going to do**
   It's not enough to have a goal. You might say to yourself, "I want to get new leads from my networking events." That's nice, but how are you going to do that? Does this mean going to three events a week? Joining the Chamber of Commerce? If you don't have a specific plan for achieving your goal, you're going to waste time wandering around, hoping that the goal will just land in your lap.

3. **Not sticking to your plan**
   If you've ever tried to lose weight, quit smoking, or begin an exercise program, you know that having a plan isn't enough. You have to stick to your plan! There are generally three reasons why a person doesn't stick to his or her plan. The first reason is they don't know how to do what they need to do. The second reason is that

they don't really want to do it. The third reason is they haven't set aside the right time on their calendar to do it. If you find yourself consistently deviating from doing what you planned to do in order to achieve your goal, take a good look at what is causing that.

4. **Over-planning**

   Although having a good plan to achieve your goal is essential, over-planning can get you off track. Let's face it. Life is what happens when you're making other plans. The difference between someone who actually achieves his or her goals and someone who does not is often the difference between someone who can adapt to circumstances and one who cannot. For example, let's say that you were planning on attending a conference, but you got stuck on a project at work. Do you just say "forget it" and go next year? No! You can get a copy of the proceedings and contact the people who went. You can read the articles and papers. You can find out if you can stream over the computer any aspects of the presentations. You have to stay flexible! When we over-plan, we fail to adapt to the circumstances that come up along the way.

5. **Engaging in time suckers**

   You know what I'm talking about. It's going to a networking event and spending the entire time near the food and drink table talking about what kind of cheese they served and where to get the best prices on chardonnay versus actively engaging in networking activities. Just showing up isn't enough.

The Top Five Things TO DO When Networking:

1. **Choose your events wisely.**

   There is an abundance of networking opportunities out there. You could easily find yourself attending events every night of the week. As I mentioned before, we introverts need time to recharge. Instead of attending every event, identify groups that will be best for your business. These are either groups of potential customers or potential partners. Once you choose one or two groups, be as active as you can! It's better to develop deep relationships with fewer people than shallow ones with many.

2. **Have an exit strategy.**

    Once you've gotten to know someone as well as you'd like, have some things you can say in advance so that you can leave the conversation. "Excuse me, I'm going to get another cup of coffee" is a good one.

3. **Approach people you know.**

    This is especially valuable when they are already talking to someone else. Don't intrude, of course, but walking up to someone you already know is a good way to get them to introduce you to someone new. "Leah! It's great to see you again. How's the real estate business?" Networking is all about relationships.

4. **Follow up with leads.**

    What's the point of getting all those business cards if you're just going to leave them in your purse? Set aside some time the next day to follow up with the people you've met. Request them as connections on LinkedIn™. Send a handwritten note. Forward an article that might be interesting to them. Then, at the next meeting, you'll have someone to talk to!

5. **Give, give, give!**

    Share business tips and success strategies. Offer to help people succeed in their business. They will remember you in the future and will be happy to refer others to you.

Building relationships through networking is much like being part of a sports team. You don't see LeBron James or Kobe Bryant winning the game all by themselves; they have to assist, rebound, and focus on inspiring and motivating the other players. It's the same thing with networking. Focus on assisting, motivating, and inspiring others to win.

Being part of a team means that when you win, everyone wins. There is no need to try and go it alone. You'll go farther if you build connections that move you in the right direction.

CEE CEE H. CALDWELL-MILLER, MA, CLC, ALS

Cee Cee H. Caldwell-Miller, also known as "The Wellness Architect," is the founder of Diamond Enterprises Int'l. Her desire is to equip you with the tools you need to live your best life every day. Cee Cee is a Personal Development and Small Business Coach, Holistic Practitioner, and the author of *Be in Good Health*. She is relentless in her quest to Empower, Encourage and Inspire people to live their Authentic Lives by Design.

Websites: http://www.mrsopportunity.info

http://www.womenofgodministries.info

http://www.diamondenterprisesintl.com

http://www.thewellnessarchitect.info

Email: mrsopportunity@gmail.com

Facebook: https://www.facebook.com/mrsopportunity

LinkedIn: www.linkedin.com/in/ceeceecaldwellmiller/

Twitter: @coachceecee

Pinterest: http://www.pinterest.com/ahealthieru

Country: USA—New Jersey—Eastern Standard Time

CHAPTER 2

NETWORKING IN YOUR NICHE

by Cee Cee H. Caldwell-Miller

As I was thinking about what to share with you regarding how to network to increase your net worth, the thought "Networking in Your Niche" came to mind. I wanted to make sure that your understanding of what we think we know to be networking is the same as mine. It's important to first understand what networking is all about according to popular opinion.

Webster's dictionary defines *networking* as the exchange of information or services among individuals, groups, or institutions; *specifically*, **it is** the cultivation of productive relationships for employment or business. This definition sounds about right to me. A niche can be explained as a distinct segment of a market. For example if you were to take the health and wellness market and narrow it down to Wellness in the Workplace, then that would be a niche. Obviously, with this definition, there are literally millions of niches known to mankind. Think about anything in your home. Just about every item falls into a specific niche. For example, your coffee table would be part of the living room furniture niche within the furniture market. If you were to take apart all the niches within the furniture market, you could probably name dozens in that one niche alone. This definition of niche is not to be confused with the one that applies to people. When somebody says he's found his niche in the world by playing basketball professionally, it means that he's found his calling. Although both use the same term, they're not the same thing at all.

For our purposes here, we're going to refer to the word *niche* as a segment of the market in which you're going to promote a product. Tangible goods are sometimes easier to wrap our heads around than a service-oriented business. They are also a lot easier to run and manage and take much less time out of your day. Think about it. If you're a copywriter, you can't just put out a book and make money over and over again. You have to write copy after copy to continue to earn a living. This translates into many hours of work. Therefore, we can define Networking in Your Niche like this: It's the exchange of information or services in a defined segment of people where relationships are formed. This sounds pretty good for the individual who looks at networking as a task to complete versus an experience to have.

When it comes down to Networking in Your Niche to me, it means networking in that segment of the market that is in alignment with your true calling in life. It is my belief that networking must come from a place of AUTHENTICITY. Here is why: I don't know about you, but I have been to numerous networking events throughout the years, and they often look the same to me. This is what happens; you have made the decision to go to a well-known networking event, because you desire to connect with like-minded individuals so that you can create your circle of influence. You take time out of your absolutely busy schedule to get dressed and commute to the stated location for what you hope to be an amazing business evening. When you get there, you enter into a room full of what appears to be powerful, progressive, friendly business people and you just know that you are going to make some awesome connections that will assist you in catapulting your business into the stratosphere. You don't want to appear pushy, aggressive, or desperate, so you casually stroll around the room, making eye contact with some people. Finally you take a seat to concoct your game plan.

You are fully aware of why you came out to the event, so after scoping out the territory, you begin the arduous task of brief introductions to those in attendance. With business cards in hand, you set out to connect with as many people as you can. The conversation usually goes a little something like this:

"Hello my name is Robin."
"My name is Lisa."
"What do you do for a living?"
"I am an accountant. And you?"
"I am a make-up artist."

You both exchange cards and move on through what seems to be an endless night of meaningless talk, but you know you must get the task done.

When the night is over and you have spoken to a myriad of people, passed out and received a great number of business cards, you feel really good about your night's accomplishments. You leave the event with much anticipation and expectation that being there will prove to be well worth your time. The next day (maybe, if then) you review the business cards and you can't believe how many people you spoke with. You fool yourself into believing that business cards = clients/referrals/money. You begin to reach out to those with whom you chatted at the event and the following happens: No answer. They don't even remember you or, if you get the chance to speak, they don't need what you are offering. This continues until you have exhausted that huge stack of cards, leaving you feeling defeated and confused about why this happened. But you don't give up; instead you persist on a merry-go-round of attending networking event after networking event because this is what you know to do to grow your business.

With that being said, if you do the same thing and expect different results, you are INSANE! Just think about it for a minute. Did Robin really expect to make great connections by passing out business cards and having two-minute conversations at this networking event as a make-up artist? I think not. Why? Because she was just at a networking event for the American Accounting Association.

Might I suggest a better alternative for you to consider, like Networking in Your Niche. Networking is connecting authentically with someone on the same heart level. Therefore, networking in your niche is simply connecting with a person authentically, out of the heart, on purpose, with the intent to create a mutually beneficial experience for both of you. Please let this sit with you for a moment. Wouldn't you rather share your time with people with whom you see yourself in partnership with throughout the years to come? Not just momentary distractions, which may move you away from your true purpose and God-designed destiny.

It is so important that you discover your niche so that you are spending your precious time and sharing your special gifts with people who are truly like-minded, in sync, and kindred souls—not just in word, but in action, purpose, and spirit. You must engage in niche research, which is the in-depth study of a segment of a market in order to determine if that market has a sufficient demand to warrant the production of the product or service that you are interested in developing and are passionate about. Remember that your time is truly valuable, so use it effectively, efficiently, and excellently. You must work Smarter not Harder to gain the business success you desire.

Robin might prefer this scenario: After defining and researching her niche, she decides to go to a networking event for the Professional Beauty Association. Now, based on the above-mentioned scenario, wouldn't you agree that this makes more sense? So now the evening goes a little something like this:

"Hello, my name is Robin."

"Hello my name is Denise. So what do you do?"

"I'm a make-up artist. What do you do?"

"I'm a beauty salon owner looking to partner with a make-up artist to expand my business."

The two sit, talk, share goals, dreams, and their visions for the future of their mutual businesses, and ultimately realize that partnering would be an answer to both of their prayers. They exchange information and set up a time to meet at a later date to further discuss a potential partnership. Although they did not get the opportunity to collect tons of business cards, they are not bothered by that at all. Why? Let me tell you: First, Robin knew her niche. She was purposeful in choosing where to go to network. She made a connection with someone who needed what she had to offer. She then took time out to get to know the lead and made a real, authentic connection. Finally, she set up a time to re-connect. I would say that this was a better use of Robin's time, wouldn't you?

When you make a heart connection, you make a genuine, lasting relationship that can lead to a profitable business relationship as well. When you are considering hitting the networking circuit, this is something we all must do to further our business goals and expand our connections. Please keep these things in mind because "Networking in Your Niche" can lead to your ability to "Network to Increase Your Net Worth."

KIOSHANA L. LACOUNT

Kioshana LaCount **is a speaker, author, and career and lifestyle coach. She currently owns and operates The Excellence Initiative, LLC, a career education and coaching firm based in Gadsden, AL. She has over 11 years of experience in working in the career services and life skills fields, teaching and empowering people both young and old to work at continually improving their lives. Her professional career spans the corporate, government and non-profit sectors, and she writes about her experiences in the career industry through her blog, "Job Snobbing".** She is a 2009 graduate of Alabama State University, where she holds an honors degree in marketing and international business.

For more information or to contact Kioshana visit:

Website: www.KioshanaLaCount.com

www.ExcellenceGED.com

www.JobSnobbing.com

Facebook: The Excellence Initiative, LLC
(http://www.facebook.com/ExcellenceInitiative)

Email: Kioshana.LaCount@gmail.com

CHAPTER 3

LEVERAGING COMMUNITY SERVICE AS A MEANS OF NETWORKING

by Kioshana L. LaCount

My first job after graduating from college was a position with my local Boys and Girls Clubs as the marketing and fundraising coordinator. The ink hadn't quite dried on my degree before I was thrust headfirst into my new job as a one-woman public relations and resource development shop for this organization. My activities supported four club sites throughout the area and, like many small- and medium-sized nonprofits in this part of the country, there were significant financial challenges. As I went about learning my position and all that it entailed, I constantly sought out opportunities for additional training. Most of the opportunities that I found were local workshops facilitated by companies that were able to host them at little or no cost as a means of corporate giving and community reinvestment. Although I cannot recall summarily the content of any of the sessions that I attended, I do remember one extremely valuable lesson that I learned during that time: Helping people can be a very lucrative business move.

This is a principle that I have seen hold true throughout my life, in many different aspects. Whether it is a Mary Kay representative providing free make-up consultations to women at a local domestic violence shelter or a financial services company providing workshops on attaining start-up funds for a business at the local library, the power of community service cannot be understated. Providing opportunities for the community to take part in your business and service offerings exposes you to a larger group of people. This expands the potential customer base past what can be reached through more traditional means of marketing. It also helps you to build credibility by allowing you to demonstrate on a larger stage exactly what you are able

28

to do and how you can add value to the personal and/or professional lives of your customers. Finally, providing these services to the community at large enables you to build goodwill within the community in which you operate. Providing these services allows people to see you as a real person instead of simply as a faceless business, and they begin to feel as though they know you. Relationship marketing or network marketing thrives on these personal connections to others in your network. There is no better way to build and expand your network than to simply get out there in front of people.

There are several ways in which business owners can integrate the idea of utilizing community service within their strategic marketing plan. The first and most common way to do this is to join an organization of professionals whose aim it is to affect positive change within the community. Examples of this are organizations such as Kiwanis or Altrusa clubs, which are nonprofits that stand alone.

Kiwanis International is a global organization of volunteers organized into local cohorts who are dedicated to networking and service within their communities. According to Kiwanis.org, in a typical year Kiwanis clubs worldwide dedicate more than 12 million hours of service to more than 150,000 service projects locally and globally.

Altrusa International is a global community service organization that focuses on improving the communities through leadership, partnership, and service. Although Altrusa strives to meet the needs of the local communities as a whole, the specific focus of the organization is literacy education. More information on Altrusa International can be found by visiting Altrusa.com.

It could also be networking organizations that are affiliated with nonprofits, such as the United Way Young Leaders Society or the Urban League Young Professionals. Although these are both examples of service organizations, each represents a different mission and value system.

The United Way Young Leaders Society is a group comprised of young professionals who are dedicated to furthering the United Way's vision of building great communities by bringing people together to help others. The organization works to develop young professionals into leaders by teaching them to work together toward a common goal. Visit your local United Way office to learn more about joining the Young Leaders Society.

The Urban League Young Professionals is an auxiliary of the Urban League, which targets young professionals, empowering them to affect positive change throughout their communities by way of the Urban League Movement. Areas of focus for this organization include education and youth empowerment, economic empowerment, health and quality of life empowerment, civic engagement, and civil rights and racial justice empowerment. Visit NULYP.net or your local Urban League chapter for more information about this great organization.

Membership in these organizations is a great networking move because it allows you to meet and get to know other like-minded individuals within your local area. Through these avenues, you will have the opportunity to network in a less structured, lower pressure environment while at the same time doing some good for those around you.

An alternative to this for someone looking for a higher profile and more involved opportunity is to become a corporate or advisory board member for the organization of your choice. This will allow professionals to apply their unique skills and talents to further the mission of their chosen program as well as assist in establishing/building credibility. Nonprofits tend to seek out professionals from all walks of life, and entrepreneurs are especially appealing because of the diversity of their skill sets. Most nonprofit boards recruit new members annually as older members retire and make room for fresh faces and new ideas. Attending open houses or chamber events with a nonprofit focus is a great way to get noticed by those who are currently on the boards you would like to join.

If the long-term commitment required by membership affiliation is not appealing to you, there are still other avenues for community involvement. As mentioned earlier, one of the best ways to do this is to partner with an organization to provide free or low-cost events for their clients or the community at large. Currently, my company, whose focus is career training and education, is developing a partnership with an after-school program to provide career development workshops for the parents of its members. I will benefit from this collaboration by building my credibility as an expert in the field of career services while also generating positive buzz about my company to a wide and diverse group of people throughout the local market. The program will benefit from the opportunity to provide a different type of service to its clients and gaining more buy-in from the community at large. Whether I receive a direct monetary profit from this arrangement is irrelevant because I will have gained an incredible amount of ground within my market in a very short time. Moreover, this will have cost me nothing but my time. This is truly a win–win situation for all involved!

Of course, there are still other opportunities for community involvement as well. Volunteering as a representative of yourself and your business for larger community events such as United Way's annual Day of Action is a great example. This event requires that you take only one day out of your busy schedule to work with a team of other volunteers to assist with projects in your community. You'll meet tons of new people, garner some positive branding for your company, and even get a free lunch out of it—what's not to love? Social media provides still other opportunities in the form of blogging, webinars, promotional campaigns—the possibilities are truly endless!

Regardless of what you decide to do, no matter how large or small the effort, know that it will have a positive effect on you as well as the people that you help. The Law of Reciprocity states that all transmissions of energy result in a return of energy in like kind. More simply, you get what you give. This is a universal truth that we have all seen demonstrated at some point in our lives. The great thing about approaching your marketing plan from an altruistic standpoint is that you are always affecting positive change in the world around you, which will in turn result in a positive change at your bottom line.

That said, go forth and (help someone) prosper!

AUDREY WOODLEY

Audrey Woodley, Founder of Changing Oasis, Inc. and FEW Entertainment, is a motivational speaker, life coach, radio talk show host and entrepreneur. Audrey has over 15 years with educating and coaching women. Audrey served on many leadership boards, Changing Oasis, Chicago Public Schools, and Order of Eastern Star. Audrey loves her pumps and she is a testimony on how she made a decision to walk in those pink pumps and get herself a life coach.

#Chicagoteachersrock #IAmAudrey #ChangingOasis

Website: www.changingoasis.org

Facebook: https://www.facebook.com/pages/Changing-Oasis-Foundation

Twitter: https://twitter.com/ChangingOasis

LinkedIn: http://www.linkedin.com/in/mzaudrey

Pinterest: http://pinterest.com/diamonds40/

CHAPTER 4

COACHING AND NETWORKING CHANGED MY LIFE AND INCREASED MY BOTTOM LINE

by Audrey Woodley

Several years ago I started Changing Oasis, Inc., a nonprofit organization. My vision and purpose was to help and empower women through proper guidance, education, training and coaching. Initially, this was a huge undertaking because in Chicago's inner city some women feel that they don't need anything except a pair of shoes, some cute lipstick and eyelashes to appear to be successful. I know because I use to think that way as well until I realized that we all needed much more than that. This became increasingly apparent once I hired my first life coach. My coach helped me to develop the skills that I needed to succeed and also helped me find the necessary resources that would guarantee my success.

Before I started Changing Oasis, my life was spiraling downward. I was at a very difficult point in my life and I was experiencing a lot of failure. I had worked many years in the Chicago Public School system only to find myself being displaced by budget cuts and layoffs even though my credentials included me having more than 15 years of experience, a Master's Degree in Leadership and a License to become a principal, yet I was still downsized. At the time I felt hurt and discouraged. But instead of letting that get me down, I decided to embrace it as a life lesson and to use the situation as a bridge to help me get over to the right side of success. I also decided to use every lesson that I had ever taught my students to help myself and build my business. I can remember telling them that failure is not an option. I remembered how I would push them to succeed and that is just the way I began to push myself.

Little by little and every calculated step-by-step, I started rebuilding not only my broken self image, but also my spiritual being. I made a conscious and wise decision to invest in a more successful and happier future for myself. So, I took the monies that I would normally allocate for shoe shopping and instead I hired a life coach. My coach taught me to focus on my inner strengths and let go of past hurts by cleaning out old baggage including family drama. Now several years later, I'm looking and feeling much better, and since I still love shoe shopping I sought out money making opportunities that allow me to shop for shoes and make money at the same time. I have an online shoe boutique called Shoe Savvy and I operate and sell shoes in association with the Nchantment online shoe store where you can shop for shoes 24/7. And, n addition to Changing Oasis, Inc. and Nchantment, I am the owner of a social media consulting company called FEW Entertainment which provides Social Media Boutique services to individuals and small businesses. My coaches have provided me with a lot of valuable information. And, if there is one important thing that every person who wants to be successful should know, it would be this: DO NOT (UNDER ANY CIRCUMSTANCES) put all of your eggs in one basket. This would include relying on any one person to help you get to the next level. For example, many of my clients are visual so I have hired several Graphic Design and Marketing specialists to help create my business advertisement. This allowed me to get my marketing materials completed by at least one of the specialists whenever needed. My ability to constantly keep my businesses active and growing has helped increase my bottom line. Basically, always put yourself in the position to sell because there is always someone willing to buy and you must be prepared to deliver!

This past year I started on a journey to increase my network and had several goals in mind. I wanted to increase awareness about my business brands, drive traffic to my special events and I wanted to generate PR buzz for my businesses. In order to achieve these goals, I decided to create what I call the *Art of Feminine Presence*, which represents the principles that I use to make a lasting impression on the people that I meet. These principles are as follows:

- Always have a headshot and your bio available because you may be asked to speak on a panel or be interviewed about your business.
- Make sure you have written two to three press releases. This will help you when someone has to introduce you and they don't have a lot of time to research all that you do.

- If you have a network, be sure to promote and send your headshot to their website, just in case someone asks you where they can get more information about you and your business. Your image and name will pop up in the Google+ web image search.

- Find ways to be a speaking expert in your field and capitalize on this opportunity by building your credibility as an expert among your peers or interested parties in your specialized industry who will be in your listening audience.

- Make sure your website is designed in a way that accurately represents your brand. If you are using a website for free, you will be very limited. If you are using Ning, you have to pay for adding events and your fees are due up front. So, if you want to get out there with little or no money, try the Wix or WordPress or create a Facebook fanpage to match and market what you're doing. Keep your fanpage updated and link it to your website. Your web presence is key to communicating your business and brand to the world.

- Create a professional business profile on LinkedIn and update it weekly using the FLIPboard App. Social media can help you build your bottom line, so it is very important that you plan your schedule and time to post updates. Keep everything current by updating daily and at a minimum updating weekly. Post pictures on your social networks that relate to your business and brand or the ideas that you want communicated to your prospective customer or client.

- Be proactive about learning new technology skills and applications that will enable you to market your business using your mobile phone. There are phone apps that will allow you to market more readily and easily. For example the FLIPboard App will allow you to access all of your social media sites in one place saving you time and energy and making you more efficient at keeping your sites fresh and current.

I utilized the previously mentioned "Art of Feminine Presence" principles as described and as a result I was able to successfully build a network of prospective clients, referral partners and increase my brand's awareness all through a plan of action that took advantage of the powerful reach of social networking. The following is a short list of my accomplishments in this area:

First, I joined the B.O.S.S. (Bringing Out Successful Sisters) network here in Chicago. Being a part of this network has allowed me to join a network of professional business women and be featured as a business woman on their members' list which is prominently displayed on their website. I use my affiliation with this organization to expand my network and build business partnerships with other Chicago-based business women. And, just like another popular site, I'm able to post, blog, add pictures and promote my events. All of this social media activity exposes my brand to hundreds of people.

Secondly, I started an online affiliated radio show with Intellectual Radio, for Changing Oasis, Inc. With stream radio I was able to create a buzz around my organization and its activities. I was able to use Changing Oasis, Inc. radio as a springboard to build a following around our message of empowerment and entrepreneurship. Our foundation's name is more recognizable today than it previously was thanks to my gig as a radio host on my own show promoting my own brand and providing other business men and women with the opportunity to reach a larger audience in promoting their brands as well. Since the radio show was national I was able to connect with other professionals outside of my usual circle of friends and business network. I built partnerships with business owners in LA, ATL, Houston, and FL. Changing Oasis, Inc radio initially began broadcasting on intellectual radio with U-Stream and then we later transitioned to producing our own shows on Bambuser. The biggest advantage to utilizing this radio streaming media is the opportunity to build your brand the way you want to and in your own timeline and at your own pace. It really is your baby and you can decide what you want it to grow up and become with little to no advertising dollars needed to accomplish such a big dream.

And last but not least, I developed a larger social media presence by creating a Fan page for my business on Facebook. As a result of creating this page many of my fans are able to see more content and communicate socially. This is something that takes a few months to build, because you have to promote by using pay per click, sponsored story, and paying a company to get your likes up. For me, I did a little of both, and I learned that you should tag your fan page whenever you're posting in any of the group message boards with which you affiliate. There are various ways to get people to participate in brand awareness campaigns which include but are not limited to: contests, free give-aways or incentive based sales like buy one and get one free.

KENDRA R. GAINEY

Kendra R. Gainey is an entrepreneur extraordinaire whose passion is to inspire women to Dare2Own! She is the proprietor and CEO of Gainey Girl Boutique, LLC, a women's specialty clothing store, and Angel Care, A Family Child Care Place, LLC. Kendra lives to inspire, encourage, and empower women to turn their hobbies into businesses that provide financial relief and stability. She believes each woman is just one step away from reaching her true potential. Kendra lives in New Jersey with her husband, Bo, and daughter.

Website:	www.GaineyGirlBoutique.com
Email:	kendra@GaineyGirlBoutique.com
Website:	www.Dare2Own.com
Email:	kendra@Dare2Own.com
Facebook:	www.Dare2Own
Facebook:	www.facebook.com/GaineyGirlBoutique.com
	www.facebook.com/Dare2own.com
Twitter:	@GaineyGirl216
Instagram:	GaineyGirlBoutique

CHAPTER 5

CONNECTING THE DOTS: THERE IS MONEY IN THE FOLLOW-UP!

by Kendra R. Gainey

So you've gone to this great networking event and you were able to get your product and/or services in front of quite a few interested potential customers. Great! Now, how do you "connect the dots" and turn those potential customers into satisfied repeat customers? You keep your word and make your follow-up calls in the 24 to 48 hours after your meeting. In doing so, you open up a potential means for income to flow to you while teaching yourself discipline in the principle of follow-up. While on the call, jot down what the customer likes about your merchandise, product, and/or services; also record something personal that stands out about your customer (contact) as this will help you cultivate an ongoing relationship.

Have you ever had a sure lead that you knew was money in the bank? You had what they wanted; all you had to do was get it to them. But you let the hours turn into days and the days into a week and when you finally got around to fulfilling the customer's need, they informed you that they got the very same product you had from someone else days ago. This, my friend, is a result of poor discipline in follow-up.

As a dreamer, doer, entrepreneur x 2 (owner of Gainey Girl Boutique, LLC, and Angel Care, A Family Child Care Place, LLC), an advocate for children, and a previous direct seller for many years who has enjoyed team building and the benefit of residual income (income that you do not have to go to work for in order to receive it), I can tell you with certainty "there is money in the follow-up." The steps that you take will determine whether or not you are the recipient of the financial reward.

Networking events and conferences are fertile ground for growing your business. You meet people in and out of your zip code that can connect you to people far beyond your circle of influence. Connecting with them and their social media outlets can make you an international hit overnight, so be specific and intentional when connecting. Social media is the best marketing for your business today because it's FREE and has the potential to reach millions—okay, billions—daily. So make good use of this reach and follow-up every tweet, every post, and every inquiry made, and watch your customer base grow as you begin to add dollars and cents to your bottom line. Remember, a virtual customer is an important customer too. Technology has made following up with customers/contacts super easy; you just need to spend some time daily or at least weekly doing it.

It's a must that you categorize your customers (contacts) and file them as soon as possible so that you remember the particulars about the contact when you begin your callbacks in the standard 24 to 48 hours. This practice will sharpen your memory and your attitude toward every contact (potential customer), and that will help you to become proficient in closing the sale or deal when the opportunity presents itself. After all, the follow-up should make dollars and cents!

Here's what I know for sure: Customer service equals customer care, and customer care equals happy, satisfied repeat customers. It's all in the follow-up. A new customer is a joy, and a repeat customer is a blessing. You need both for increase. I'll also share this nugget with you from my direct selling days: Gaining and retaining will keep you growing. In other words, adding new customers while retaining the old customers will grow your business always. You want to gain and retain—it's a sign that your business is alive and well.

In a nutshell, my friend, if you are a business owner of a brick and mortar store, an online store, a caterer, a nonprofit, a consultant with a direct selling company, or any other business that you want to take to the next level, networking and follow-up are the keys to your lifeline. Sales and deals are brokered every day outside the office. Chance meetings are no accidents, they are opportunities, so always be ready with your 30-second commercial. Think of it this way: lights, camera, sell! You must NETWORK to INCREASE YOUR NET WORTH. People will buy from you because they like what you have to offer and they relate to you on some level. Your product knowledge, your availability, your willingness to share, and your attitude are your tools, so keep them sharpened and always ready.

If your goal is to build a strong repeat customer base through networking, then you should follow these simple rules:

- Tap into your passion; know your product and make sure that you're always ready because you only have 30 seconds—lights, camera, sell!
- Join your local NETWORKING CHAPTER and get ACTIVE.
- Use social media to GROW, promote, and showcase your business.
- Support and encourage others: There is a gift in giving.
- Follow up, follow up, follow up—say what you mean and mean what you say.

It's just that simple. There is no magic formula or get-rich-quick scheme. There is just good ol' solid hard work and a few great connections. That's the recipe for success! That's why your mom always said to be nice to EVERYONE because they just might be the help you need. Keep that thought in mind when networking. Not everyone will be the help or sale you're looking for, but they could be connected to the person you're looking for, so always be courteous and follow up. Who knows what will come out of the contact? In addition, recommendations are priceless in the world we live in today.

Okay so now it's your time. You've got the insight, you've planned, you've researched, and you've prayed. It's time for you to walk into your greatness. You're an entrepreneur who is armed and ready. It's time to NETWORK to INCREASE YOUR NET WORTH. It's time to build your customer base because you now know the importance of follow-up. It is vital if you want the benefit of dollars and cents! Get your calendar out if you're like me or your iPad or your smart phone—whatever your preference is—and pull out your customer list (contacts). Start calling and reconnecting. Reintroduce yourself. Let them know what you have going on and how it can benefit them and ask for referrals.

Spend an hour making calls, then recap, reorganize, and purge your list to see where you are. You'll be surprised at what a little determination will accomplish. You probably will end up saying to yourself, "Look how easy that was in just an hour." Now you have new sales and leads too! Yes! There is money in the follow-up. Continue to make calls. You might hear a no or not right now from time to time, but don't let it deter you. Simply move forward to the next call. There is a yes waiting for you!

Now that you've made your calls, your phone probably won't stop ringing because the word is out about how great your merchandise, product, and/or services are and how your customer care is second to none. You've seen a great increase in your business sales, and your profit margin is rising steadily, so keep the momentum—don't stop! Make follow-up part of your daily routine. Every day you should make no fewer than 5 calls, send 5 emails, and take to social media, including Facebook, Twitter, Instagram, and LinkedIn, just to name a few. Communicate at least once daily. The more active you are with social media, the more response you'll get, which will definitely increase your customer base and help grow your profit margin.

Now that you are charged up, armed, and ready, I'll share another nugget with you: Invest in yourself, network with style, prepare in advance, and be a student who is ready to learn. Remember to make consistent efforts and follow up, follow up, follow up!

Connecting the dots is necessary if you wish to see your follow-up translate into dollars and cents. My advice to you is never leave a lead unturned as the one you miss could very well be the surprise that you've been waiting for.

Remember that there is no entrepreneur who is basking in the glow of financial wealth that got there overnight. What you see took years— sometimes decades—to attain, so don't compare your life or business to anyone else's. Set your goals, be flexible, always add balance to everything you do, and forge ahead. Your time is now! My question to you is will you win, place, or show? Please say that you're an entrepreneur who is in it to WIN!

Networking is a big part of my life and an even bigger part of my businesses. To be honest, it comes with its own set of challenges, but the rewards have been greater! I've been able to build a network of supportive, like-minded people who have helped keep me focused and goal conscious. My biggest lesson has been that there is definitely money in the follow-up. You will learn this lesson too as soon as you begin to practice these simple techniques. Good luck, my friend, and know that I am over here cheering for you and wishing you all the best.

KIM MCCARTER

Kim McCarter is a branding and social media strategist, coach, and speaker. As a plus-size fashion blogger, she developed a branding strategy that allowed her to learn what it took to build her blog through the eyes of her readers. By taking the core techniques of business and the evolving use of social media, she was able to develop innovative strategies that uniquely skyrocket businesses through the social media platforms that consumers are using daily. Kim graduated from DeVry University in 2010 with a bachelor's degree in business administration and has more than a decade of experience in high-level customer service and social interactions. She currently resides in northern New Jersey.

Facebook: https://www.facebook.com/bornsocialllc

Facebook: www.facebook.com/MsKimMcCarter

Twitter: https://www.twitter.com/bornsocialllc

LinkedIn: http://www.linkedin.com/in/kimmccarter

Website: www.born-social.com

Website: www.kimmccarter.com

CHAPTER 6

PUT IT IN YOUR PURSE (NETWORKING JEWELS TO SUCCESS)

by Kim McCarter

Some of us are just born to network, and some are not. I am what some would call a natural "people person"; however, that does not make me exempt from obtaining the skills necessary to effectively network and grow professionally. In my world, everyone is a customer, and it has been that way for more than 20 years. I started in customer service as a cashier in high school and literally worked my way through the ranks until I managed a call center. When I co-founded my blog in 2009, I was surprised by the fact that it instantly created an atmosphere that drew readers from far outside of my regular circle of friends. At the time, the social media industry was just starting to take off and I relied on it heavily to grow our online presence. It was in this process that I realized (although not instantly) just how much I love social media. So what I did was combine my education in business with my experience in customer service to create a powerful blog. The rest is history.

As a blogger, I began to work with several plus-size brands that were looking to strengthen their social media presence. Believe it or not, our blog is not driven by daily content. In fact, sometimes it can be over a month before we write a blog post. Nevertheless, that does not seem to stop businesses from constantly reaching out to inquire about my services. It was while developing these business relationships that other bloggers started to take notice. Some began to wonder and even ask how I came to know so many people from the plus-size industry. The people I know range from executives in leading plus-size brands to numerous plus-size models who have graced major runways and the covers of major print campaigns and television ads. I also know many of the top plus-size bloggers—and the best part is that I know them all on a first-name basis. Not to toot my own horn, but I am more than a face they recognize; these people know me. They remember our last interaction and me. When folks ask me how I was able to do this, my answer has always been the simplest word: networking. I learned to network in such a way that it has allowed my colleagues and potential customers to remember me. Do not get me wrong. It was not easy, and not everything worked. However, over time, I took notice, kept notes, and began constructing my golden list of networking jewels. If something worked, I hung on to it; when it did not, I replayed the conversations over and over in my mind, realizing where the conversation went wrong and developing various scenarios to enrich the exchange should I ever get a second opportunity.

Although I cannot go into detail about everything I have learned, I can share with you some of my most important (and often outside of the box) tricks I have learned to make networking a success. I like to call them jewels, and they go a little something like this:

Jewel #1: Printed Marketing Material—Never Leave Home Without It!

Out of everything I will share with you, this is the most obvious: printed marketing materials. Whether you have a business card or postcard, you should never leave home without printed contact materials. When investing in your marketing materials, make sure your design is eye-catching and represents exactly what you want it to say to the public. It should be consistent with your logo and website design. Your business card should include these key elements: your name, title, phone number, an email address, social media links, website address, and the physical address of your business, if applicable. Depending on your industry, a standard business card is sufficient. However, you may feel the need to invest in 3x5 postcards as well. If you invest in both, an important thing to remember when handing out your marketing materials is your environment. There is no need to hand out a 3x5 postcard at a cocktail mixer. Unlike women, men do not carry handbags, and the women will more than likely be carrying a small handbag that coordinates with their ensemble. The worst feeling in the world is seeing your marketing materials tossed around unwanted and used as coasters. If you are opening your business on a shoestring budget, there are online shops available that will offer free business cards. But the downside to this option is that, with every business card you pass out, you will end up advertising their online printing business as well.

Jewel #2: Know Your Customer!

Spend time getting to know your audience, but make sure to research who really needs your business services. A major misconception is that a business can be all things to all people. This is not true. Are you a business to consumer business or a B2B? Ask yourself, who does your product serve? Leave behind the mindset that it is okay to sell ice to an Eskimo and truly take the time to develop your business around a customer base that will allow growth. I cannot stress this enough: RESEARCH, RESEARCH, RESEARCH the type of customer you want to reach. By researching your targeted audience, you will be able to classify your business and develop your niche. A thousand businesses can offer the same services as you, but once you have taken the time to understand the needs of the customer; it will make a huge difference in whether they do business with you or your competitor. Knowing your customer eases the direction of business meetings and cold pitching. It will assist you in answering questions and speaking with your potential customer rather than at them.

Jewel #3: Know Your Story!

You should know and fully understand your pitch. I know I touched on this briefly in my second jewel, but developing a business pitch can be easier said than done. The last thing you want to do is sound like a rehearsed chorus line. I developed my HERstory by replaying the questions that were always asked and combining them with the unasked. How did you get started? What exactly do you offer? What makes your business different? How can your business help improve their bottom line? Do you have a niche in your field? What makes you an authority? I know it seems like a lot, but guess what? Wouldn't these be the same questions you would want answers to before hiring another business for your brand? Of course, you would. Not only is it important to know the answer to these questions, but it is equally important to speak them fluently and in such a way that they naturally flow. In addition, if there is ever a question you truly cannot or would rather not answer, there is no harm in advising a potential client that you will get back to them once you research it further. Trust me, getting back to a client with the correct information will put you in a much better position than having to recant whatever you previously stated.

Jewel #4: Use Your Ears!

Learn to listen. Do not become so focused on delivering your message that you miss the opportunity to understand the needs of your potential customer. The customer wants to be heard. There were countless times during my call center days when a customer would call in just to have their story heard. If you are not listening, you will be unable to make sure you are meeting their needs—or even have the skills to. The inability to listen can cost you a great contract opportunity. Even worse, it can put you in a contract that you dread.

Jewel #5: Get Excited!

Speak with enthusiasm and a smile. Although it is always important to maintain your professionalism, it is okay to share your passion for your business with your potential customer. Customers enjoy working with a business that has a passion for their field. This concept is very similar to having a disgruntled cashier at a department store. The line is moving slow. The cashier is working at a snail's place, and the negative energy begins to work its way through the line. By the time you get to the counter, you are just as annoyed as the cashier looks. In the back of your mind you think, "why are you here if you hate it so much?" (even though you know for some they may not have a choice). Do not become that cashier at any point of your presentation and/or conversation. Remember: Unlike that cashier, this is YOUR business and the monetary bottom line affects YOU.

Jewel #6: Develop your professional confidence!

As I mentioned before, I have worked for 20 years in the customer service field. Believe me when I tell you that I have fumbled my way through a dozen presentations simply because I was nervous or unsure of myself. Take time to get to know your professional self. Practice in the mirror or in front of family members. Avoid the use of repetitive words such as "umm," "okay," and "you know what I mean." Speak of your service and/or product with pride. Dress appropriately and make sure you are neatly groomed. Allow your confidence to speak for itself, but do not allow pride to overshadow it. There is a thin line between pride and confidence. I can count on one hand the number of people who will do business with someone who is arrogant, and I can multiply that number by 10 to discover the number of people who will sign a contract with someone who is not confident in their abilities to get the job done. You own your success do not destroy it.

Jewel #7: Wear Comfortable Shoes!

Your shoes should always be comfortable. This jewel will probably raise some eyebrows, but think about it: Have you really thought about how the discomfort of a pair of shoes can control everything in your immediate train of thought? There is nothing more embarrassing than discussing your business with a potential customer and you're wiggling. You become more focused on your discomfort than on getting to your customer. An extra tip for female entrepreneurs: Purchase a pair of folding ballet shoes from your local drug store and keep them in your purse. You will thank me later.

As you can see, the keys to successful networking can take an eclectic mix of traditional and non-traditional approaches. More often than not, we become so focused on the fundamentals of building our business that we can forget the simplest things that can make a difference. Take time to master the basic skills of networking and then develop them to truly meet your needs. Trust me when I tell you that, once the foundation is set, the rest will be a breeze!

ROSEMARIE COUTURE DESARO

Roe DeSaro is the voice for inspiring strong, competent, high-achieving women to achieve success without compromising their family and personal life, while being their authentic feminine self. Her expertise comes from 34 years of award winning achievements as a large firm Corporate VP executive, a Wall Street partner, an Independent Sales professional, and a Small Business entrepreneur. Her company, Fearless in Pink, provides coaching, speaking, master minding & success programs. From Bond Broker to Stockbroker to FunBroker, she is creating more fun, freedom and fulfillment in other people's lives. Today she is known as the Queen of the "Stress-Free SuperWoman".

Best Selling Author ~ Empowering Transformations for Women

Websites: www.FearlessInPink.com

www.StressFreeSuperWoman.com

www.SuccessWithNoSacrifice.com

Facebook: Facebook.com/FunBroker

Twitter: Twitter.com/FunBroker

LinkedIn: LinkedIn.com/FunBroker

Email: Roe@Fun-N-Wealth.com

Contact: 1-800-380-9097

CHAPTER 7

CREATE JOINT VENTURES FOR ACCELERATED RESULTS

by RoseMarie Couture DeSaro

*I can do what you can't do and you can do what
I can't do. Together we can do great things.*
–Mother Teresa

*If we both do the same thing and bring our
strengths to the table, together we can
achieve milestones.*
–RoseMarie Couture DeSaro

Thirty minutes into the webinar, 100 people signed up for the program being offered at $1997. By the time the purchase cart was closed, it had registered 302 new enrollees. Now do the math. That's more than $600,000 earned in the blink of an eye! Mind-blowing to say the least. The power of these two experts working together was mesmerizing. I, of course, became one of their 300+ new clients. The value they brought to the table was just irresistible. This is the power of joint ventures. What I witnessed is what's called a home run in the joint venture (JV) world. It was way beyond affiliate marketing! The art of promotional partnerships unveiled itself to me that day, and it literally changed the course of my life forever!

Joint Ventures Defined

So, what exactly is a JV? Or promotional partnership? In simplicity, it's a collaborative effort with another person or group of people with a specific goal or goals that can serve each other's success in several ways. Initially, one would think to simply increase profits. Other benefits range from expanding your business, credibility, and center of influence; building your list, and delivering a great service/benefit, which is what I witnessed that day on the webinar. The goals for each partner can be completely different from one another. For example, your expert partner already has a huge influence and following while you have a great product idea that is unique and would resonate well with their list. Here, the expert partner gets to provide value to their existing clients and expand their list even more while you get exposure and sales that could have taken years to develop. Some JV partners want value more than income, some want to serve their clients, some want to promote their products, and some want it all—profits, promo, exposure, and added value. The ultimate goal and sure winner is obviously when it's a win–win–win for all involved: a win for you, a win for your JV partner, and a win for the consumer. Take a look at this book collaboration, for example. It's a JV: a group of experts coming together to share their expertise. The authors benefit by gaining exposure, credibility, and influence. The readers benefit by gaining knowledge at an affordable price. Other examples are teleseminars, joint webinars, workshops, vendors' expos, radio/TV shows, etc. *It can be local and/or online.* In my experience, to create the largest leverage and success and have a grand slam event, online is the way to go, although I enjoy doing both because I still love the face-to-face aspect of my business. If you're not a people person like me, then this can be achieved 100% online. Think global domination. Obviously it all depends on your type of business. By now though, you get the picture. The main ingredient is that the value has to be huge for *everyone* involved.

Steps to JV Success

As with any successful project, first determine your goal/vision. What do you want to achieve in both the short-term and the long-term? If you're new, building your list is important. At some point you will also need to create revenues, right? So think about what avenues you can take with a JV partner that can pay you profits—and don't forget about bringing in recurring revenues! That's where the big money is and, just as important, your time freedom. I was recently approached by a coach whose specialty was in relationships. A relationship coach was not someone on my radar, but I kept my mind open. It wasn't long before my mind started to see possibilities that never occurred to me. As I'm all about success with no sacrifice, she began to tell me stories of women putting off seeking love due to a lack of time or simply being too stressed out to deal with it. We clearly share some of the same clientele. Today, we are forming a teleseminar series that is debuting this winter. We are creating interview videos of each other, which we can use on our websites for added value. She is also creating a video training program for my clients that I can include in my Stress-Free SuperWoman expert interview series. This will create additional revenues for both of us. These ideas were created during two phone calls!

How many JV partnerships would you want? I recommend at least four per year for a newbie, but that will increase to as many as one or two per month. Your money list should consist of JV partners that are of similar stature and experience as you as well as JV partners that in your wildest dreams you would love to work with but didn't think you stood a chance. This is the time to take the bull by the horns, or as I say to my female cohorts: put your big girl panties on. I am working with individuals who are my mentors. Hey, it's a wild ride, but someone has to take it. Actually the process is quite simple, as you'll see below, because it's all about the win–win–win scenario. When deciding who your ideal partner is, see who in this world is already talking to your ideal audience. Their clients are your ideal clients. Who are they? Some checkpoints can be: Is your product/service relevant to their clients and of great value? Can you engage in cross-exposure? What are their reputation, credibility, and center of influence? Also, ask yourself "who believes in me?" Then ask for an introduction.

The next step is to approach your potential partners. This is a time when emails work! In person works too! Utilize the basic rules of networking. Make it about them. Sincere compliments are a great way to start. Ask yourself what is in it for them. Then ask them, how can I support you? There are several chapters in this book where you can get details on networking. Whether you are talking in person or sending an email, don't talk about your product and how it can blah, blah, blah. JV partners don't care about how you are going to change the world unless they are involved. Whatever you do, keep it short. Get creative. Recently I had someone send an intro via video—how's that for standing out in the crowd?! Make sure what you are asking is simple for them, have a "done for you" proposition. This is a must for approaching top influencers.

Once you have your potential partner on the phone, sit back and let the magic happen. As you are coming from that place of support, share your passion, energy, and vision while remaining open minded. Be curious. Be patient. Most of all, be unattached to the outcome. Above all, remember the old adage: Some will, some won't—so what! As always, the fortune is in the follow-up. Consistency wins the race.

Final Thought

That "home run" webinar might have opened my eyes and mind forever, but when I really think about it, I have been doing promotional partnerships and joint ventures my whole career. My claim to fame started back in 1985 while working on Wall Street. I was working among the most successful stockbrokers in the New York area. I was the only female and half their age, and I had a tall order to deliver on my contract. In New Jersey there was a stockbroker who was extremely successful selling my product. I noticed he had a huge ego and was well liked. I invited him to speak at all my branch offices, and sales began to skyrocket. The rest of the country wanted to know how I was doing it, so I made a video (8-mm, to date myself) of him on his "how to's." That year we went from $10 million in sales to $100 million. It was a win–win–win–win partnership. He became famous, I was perceived as an expert and became a VP, and my company made out like a bandit. Even the investors received a one-year 15% return. Everyone made money and lots of it. I was a "nobody" who knew "somebody" and became an icon. It was epic. So I ask you: Who do you know? Make joint venture partners a part of your business and watch your profits soar.

Oh, that coaching program—the one I joined with 300+ people on that "home run" webinar—well, they are offering it again. This time I get to partner up with them and share their program with my center of influences. If you had said I was going to partner up with two seven-figure income earners just a month ago, I would have said "yeah right"—maybe 10 years from now. At the release of this book, it may still be available.

All our dreams can come true, if we have the
courage to pursue them.
Walt Disney

MINDY BARNETT

Mindy Barnett is a holistic health and wellness coach based in Woodbridge, New Jersey. As president and founder of Nourish Your Potential, LLC, Mindy shows professionals and entrepreneurs how to make their health and well-being a priority so that they can serve more people and operate at their full potential. She is also the co-organizer of Employee to Entrepreneur, a networking group based in New York City that brings together women transitioning from the corporate world to entrepreneurship.

Website: http://nourishyourpotential.com/

Facebook: https://www.facebook.com/NourishYourPotential

Twitter: https://twitter.com/NYPWellness

LinkedIn: http://www.linkedin.com/in/mindygordonbarnett

CHAPTER 8
DITCH THE PITCH!
by Mindy Barnett

If you've ever been to a networking event, you have undoubtedly encountered people who respond to the obligatory "What do you do?" question with the following:

"I'm a (insert title here) who works with (insert target market here) who are/ have (insert problem here) and want to (insert benefit here) so that they can (insert result here) without (insert sacrifice here)."

Um...huh?

Or perhaps you yourself have used this elevator pitch formula to describe what you do. How have people responded to you? Do they express interest and inquire further about your services? Or do their eyes glaze over? Do they say, "Oh, that's nice" and make a bee-line for the bar?

I can tell you from personal experience that I have received a little more of the latter than the former. That's why I recommend that you **ditch the pitch**.

Gasp!

You may be thinking, "But my business coach/mentor and numerous networking experts *insist* that I *must* have an elevator speech so I can describe what I do at any given opportunity!"

I totally get it. My business coaches and mentors have all strongly recommended this to me as well and have offered "formulas" for creating an elevator pitch to take the mystery out of what to say. Mind you, I'm not suggesting you don't have some sort of pitch at all to arm yourself with at any given function, be it networking or otherwise. I'm just saying that you don't need to memorize and recite a lengthy, convoluted run-on sentence to explain what you do or what your business is.

Although elevator speech blueprints are all well-intentioned (and even work for some people), long formulaic pitches tend to create glazed-over glances and confusion. They can sound and feel too "sales-y" and over-rehearsed, and afterwards the person you're talking to still has no idea what you do. I'm sure those of you who have gone to many networking functions have experienced this in one way or another from either side of the conversation.

Again, I am not against elevator pitches (or cocktail lines as they are sometimes referred to). Crafting a pitch within a defined formula helps you to gain clarity on your mission and purpose in your business. Knowing who you serve, what problems you solve for those you serve, how you solve those problems, and the benefits your clients receive as a result is crucial to marketing yourself.

So why would you not want to blurt this all out to anyone you encounter at a networking function? I mean, you want to give people the full scope of what you do, right?

In certain situations, yes, a more detailed description of what you do is certainly in order. These situations include when you're presenting a workshop or are a featured speaker at an event or even in a more formalized setting such as a BNI (Business Networking International) meeting. This is also a good starting point for fleshing out copy for your marketing materials and website.

However, if you are attending a networking event that has a more social aspect to it (i.e., with cocktails and crudités), your "pitch" needs to be more relaxed while still conveying what your business is. In these particular situations, you want to entice the people you're talking with to inquire further about what you do. This strikes up a conversation and leads to developing a relationship with that person. And at the end of the day, that's what networking is all about, right?

So how do you communicate your message in a simple, yet authentic way? And what if you don't have any resemblance of an elevator/cocktail pitch to begin with? Here are the essential things you must know to get started:

1. **Who is your client?** What is the demographic (male/female, age, occupation, married/single, kids/no kids, etc.)? What are their challenges? What mistakes have they made? What keeps them up at night? What problem do they have that they'd be willing to pay

to solve? Where do they hang out? What books, magazines, blogs, etc., do they read?

2.   **What is your offer?** What problems do you solve? What results do your clients get from working with you?

Again, your answers to these questions don't all need to be in your pitch, it's just a good idea to know this like the back of your hand for when people inquire further about what it is you offer. All you need from the answers you give to these questions is the **who** and the **what**. For example:

"I'm a health coach who works with stressed-out, over-worked professionals who seek to live beyond the status quo."

"I'm a career coach who helps professionals transition from their corporate jobs to entrepreneurship."

"I show creative professionals how to achieve mental clarity and remove blocks."

"I'm a professional organizer who helps stay-at-home moms create a sane and orderly home."

"I help solo entrepreneurs coordinate workshops and seminars without hassle."

"I support recent college graduates in creating and living a life that they love."

You may be tempted to describe **how** you deliver results. Typically, that's something that the other person can ask you, should they be interested, or can be experienced directly by those who book an initial consultation with you (which is likely one of your goals with attending networking functions in the first place, correct?). Introducing the "how" in your introduction will just create a slippery slope of ramblings on and defeat the purpose of the "anti-pitch" pitch. This would also create an issue in a speed networking environment when you have a limited amount of time to talk about yourself (very much like a speed dating scenario).

You might also be inclined to pare down your pitch too much. One of the things I hear from time to time when meeting people is "I'm just a coach," or "I'm just an accountant," and so on. First of all, saying you are "just" anything diminishes your value to both the person to whom you're speaking and yourself. Embrace your unique and wonderful self and show confidence in your pitch! As with some of the examples above, you don't even necessarily have to mention your title or occupation at all. If you feel that saying you're an accountant sells you short on what you actually do, you can start with how you serve others in this role, such as "I give small business owners peace of mind by organizing their finances/books/taxes, etc." This tells people what you actually do instead of stating an over-generalized title. Crafting your pitch in this fashion works particularly well with those with more ambiguous titles, such as a "coach" or "healer," but make sure you are specific in what you do and who you serve. Statements like "I make dreams come true" or "I heal the world" are a little too vague and need further clarification.

So what happens when you're on the other end of a mile-long elevator pitch? Rather than nodding politely and conjuring up an excuse in your head to move as quickly to the other side of the room as humanly possible, listen to what the person is saying and repeat back to the person a summarized version of what you heard (very much like how you would pare down your own pitch). Even if you have little interest in what the person does, this will show the other person that you "get" her and might even inspire her to pare down her pitch as you've shown that it doesn't need to be all that complicated and wordy (what a relief!).

For example, if someone rambles off a lengthy pitch, much like the one at the beginning of this chapter, you could respond with "So, in other words, you're a speech coach who works with C-level executives on their presentations, correct?" And when the other person concurs, you can either inquire further about her business or, better yet, let her know about anyone you might know who could use her services. Some of the best networking contacts I've made have been referral partners rather than actual clients.

This also works wonderfully the other way around. Once you've dazzled someone with your streamlined pitch, there's a chance that that someone might not be anywhere in the vicinity of your ideal client profile. If this is the case, follow up with "Who do you know who could benefit from my services/products?" Not only does this make for a fruitful conversation (and not a waste of time), but it also empowers the other person by showing that you value her as a worthy referral source.

Remember, networking functions are not forums in which to regurgitate lengthy sales swill or throwing as many business cards in people's hands as possible (that's a whole other topic in itself). Networking events exist to bring together professionals and entrepreneurs so that they can build relationships. The way to do this effectively is to communicate your business, purpose, service, or product authentically and with clarity. Don't overwhelm yourself with memorizing a long "script" that would be much better suited to your autobiography. Just arm yourself with your streamlined pitch and be your wonderful, amazing, powerful, and confident self!

CATHRYN CLARKSON FINLEY

A native of Dallas, Texas Cathryn became a serial entrepreneur in the early ninety's both in business and professionally. After traveling throughout the United States and Internationally as a Product Education Trainer and Developer for Amway Artistry Cosmetics a billion dollar network marketing company and for the Mortgage Industry as a Contract Mortgage Underwriter she subsequently began her network marketing career on a part-time basis.

Today , Cathryn is an Associate with Ignite, marketing deregulated energy a life essential service that everyone uses. Energy fits into everyone's budget, people pay for it every single month and she is empowered helping other people succeed while building a residual income that you can depend on.

Cathryn's enthusiasm is contagious and her message of what it takes to succeed not only in business but also in life is a message about making a choice. Her favorite quote is "Everything you want is right outside your comfort zone."

Visit Cathryn on line at: www.mfinley.igniteinc.biz

Email: finley3and10@gmail.com

Facebook: Cathryn Finley

Pinterest: http://pinterest.com/cfinley180

CHAPTER 9

HOW TO ACE YOUR NETWORKING EVENT BEFORE YOU EVEN GET THERE

by Cathyrn Clarkson Finley

Whether you're starting your own business or transitioning to a new job, *networking* can be your life support. I was once told by a mentor of mine in the Network Marketing Industry to treat networking as if you were cooking your ideal "gumbo recipe." In order to really do this, you must incorporate a select set of ingredients that will give you that "wow" factor (taste). You want your gumbo to leave a lasting impression for all the right reasons. In other words, **You want people to keep asking you for more gumbo!**

To develop lasting relationships when networking, what I have personally experienced is that it's important to be genuine in all actions. You must listen, be patient, and understand the needs of others—while also understanding your own needs.

In order to demonstrate this, let's say that it's the middle of the week and you just received an invite to *another* networking event. After scanning over the invite from the hosts, glancing at the venue information and description, you ask yourself, "Is it worth it?" Well, here is how to make sure that it is worth it:

There are four aces that we need to trump in order to Ace Your Networking Event before you even arrive:

1. Ace of Diamonds: Network with Purpose
2. Ace of Hearts: Research—Be Informed
3. Ace of Clubs: Dress for Success
4. Ace of Spades: Be memorable and use your business cards like a credit card

Ace of Diamonds: <u>Network with Purpose</u>

Several networking events take place each day. All networking functions come with a price: *time*. Your time is valuable, so always make sure to examine your worth and ask yourself is it worth it? You have to assess key reasons as to why you need to be there. There should be a purpose. If you don't have much time to give, you should never spread yourself too thin by going to the wrong places. You need to select appropriately. Here is how to choose which networking events to attend:

- **Industry:** What industry is this function appealing to? Is this event known to provide a diverse set of professionals? Always ask yourself, "What are my needs?" Do you prefer a simple mix and mingle or one that highlights guest speakers on topics you care about? If you have a desire to sharpen certain skills, you might lean toward events that highlight expert speakers, panel discussions, or seminars that address your topics of concern. Increase your chances.

- **Cost:** Spending a lot of money does not always equate to a positive correlation with the quality of your networking experience. Have you heard the saying, "Don't judge a book by its cover?" Well, don't judge a networking function's quality by its price only.

- **Testimonials:** What's the buzz? Successful networking functions usually like to highlight previous events through featured testimonials, reviews, or photos. A picture is worth a thousand words. In the age of social media, you can usually find ways to track conversations about an event from a retweet, like, or yes—a hashtag.

- **Substance:** People often select networking socials based on their structure to determine if they align best to their professional or personal needs. Let's revisit that question you should always ask yourself: "What are my needs?"

Ace of Hearts: <u>Research—Be Informed</u>

Now that you've narrowed down your choices of networking events to attend this month, everything seems great. What do you do next? You fact find. Strategic networking practices work best when you have a limited amount of time to make your mark—the best impression—which is often the case.

- **Host/Sponsors:** Who is hosting this event? Who are their sponsors? It's always good to know their background information. You might pick up on similarities, which could lead to a great conversation. Just one conversation can lead to a valued business relationship. The hosts at events are usually busy, which is why the few moments you have with them should be meaningful. After all, they're not just hosting the event for you. They have to cater to other guests too. Make your mark.

- **Guest List:** If you're lucky, some events post the guest list of those attending their functions ahead of time. You can quickly see individuals who might be within or outside of your industry. You don't need to memorize the entire list or where each person comes from. You can make a mental note of three to five people who you definitely want to speak to. Perhaps the host's assistants could connect you prior to or during the event to your guest of interest.

- **Panel Discussion/Guest Speakers/Seminars:** I truly enjoy networking events that include a panel discussion. It's a huge bonus to receive a lesson, advice, or talk from an industry expert. Usually the theme or topics are released to guests prior to the event.

Ace of Clubs: <u>Dress For Success (wear a "conversation starter" without breaking your wallet)</u>

I recently had a conversation with a friend who said, "Why are you so dressed up? The attire on the invite said business casual." Personally, I did not consider myself dressed up at the time. So that was just me being me. I understood what this was all about after flipping through the pages of the July 2012 Issue of <u>O, The Oprah Magazine</u>. I came across an interesting study cited within the article entitled "When Envy Strikes." It said, "Whether you like it or not, most people are automatically sizing up the crowd—who's smarter, who's tougher, who's more beautiful," says Dr. Richard Smith, PhD, editor of the anthology *Envy: Theory, and Research.* More relevant to networking situations, researchers found that strangers start to assess each other immediately once they're in a room. Just knowing that attendees will be sizing up the room is reason enough to always look your best. You will want to stand out from the crowd.

Ace of Spades: <u>Be Memorable—Treat your business card like a credit card, give by connection not by sight</u>

Who has enough business cards to start their own collectibles? Some of the cards in my collection come from designs by Staples, <u>Vistaprint</u>, and Office Max. One thing for sure is that they're not my own business cards! These cards are viewed like connections waiting to happen.

In my comings and goings I've discovered that networking is about building genuine connections with people. It should not be about dispersing as many promotional materials to as many people as you can see in the room. However, I must admit that many of these cards are the best conversation starters.

In networking, you should take the time to listen as much as you take the time to speak. Some enthusiastic networkers might forget this and occupy 95% of the conversation, making it completely one-sided. In these circumstances, relationships are rarely built. You won't have any knowledge of your listener's needs, wants, and passions. You might find it frustrating because you weren't able to detect similarities to build support, friendships, or partnerships. And you couldn't do that because you did all the talking. So don't be that networker. It's very tacky.

Now that you have your four aces, use them to your advantage and you will ACE your networking activities every time.

JAYNE RIOS

Jayne Rios is an entrepreneurial leader who inspires and coaches others to achieve unlimited success in the digital world. She is the Founder and CEO of three successful companies including KungFuzos Video, Acts 2 Technology and Express Yourself eLearning. Jayne has 25 years of experience in video and marketing. She is an advocate for women entrepreneurs and is passionate about helping others achieve their dreams. Jayne lives in Dallas, TX with her husband and two sons.

Websites: www.kungfuzos.com

www.acts2technology.com

www.expressyourselfelearning.com

Telephone: 885-456-9876.

Email: Jayne@expressyourselfelearning.com

Facebook: www.facebook.com/KungFuzosMarketing

www.facebook.com/expressyourselfelearning

CHAPTER 10

INCREASE SALES AFTER NETWORKING EVENTS WITH MY SECRET WEAPON

by Jayne Rios

Simply attending networking events will not help you grow your business and increase sales. It's all about the follow-up and building those relationships after the initial meeting. I built my company to six figures by attending networking events in person, communicating often through my social media sites, and following up with my "secret weapon": video!

Video is the number two tool for generating leads and connecting with your audience after a networking event. My entire team follows a process that enables us to connect with our prospects and customers through the power of video. And now I am going to teach you our tricks!

How many events do you attend and leave with tons of cards and new contacts? A lot I would imagine, if you are making networking a priority. Of these contacts, how many faces and personalities do you remember? There might be a memorable few, but the rest are a blur. A typical follow-up plan consists of placing the new contacts into an email system and sending a generic "Great to meet you" email. This is the old way of doing things and doesn't further your relationships with new contacts.

The plan I am going to show you now will not only be your secret weapon, but will also set you miles ahead of your competition and shorten the sales funnel cycle.

STEP 1:

Collect cards as you connect with prospects during the networking event. Remember to jot down a note or two about your conversation. I suggest one business note and one personal note. (You will use this later.) Another great tip is to fold the corner of the business cards for the people you personally connected with and those you have a chance for an immediate appointment. These contacts will be your priority follow-ups.

STEP 2:

Prepare for follow-up. When I say prepare I mean PREPARE! A generic follow-up doesn't help a contact remember who you are. To prepare, use the following steps.

- Separate cards into hot, warm, and soft leads. The hot leads are the priority cards, with folded corners. Warm leads are contacts that have synergy with the services your company provides. Soft leads are those people who might not be a good prospect for you, but might know people who need your service. **TIP:** Don't waste your time following up with those who are not a good fit; concentrate on connecting with and forming relationships with your hot and warm leads!

- Research: The next step in preparing for follow-up is researching your hot leads. Look for ways your company can assist the prospect; check out their website, and look for press releases. Did they have a merger? Was your contact recently promoted? Has their company won an award recently? The more knowledgeable you are about the person you are writing or calling, the easier it is to connect with them at their level.

- Put yourself in the right mindset to follow up! Set a time and place where you will have no distractions. Concentrate on the goals you have set for that contact. Is it an appointment? Is it to send additional information? Is it to influence the influencer? What outcome do you want to achieve?

STEP 3:

Now we are ready to use my secret weapon: video! Based on the feedback I have received, video is the number one tool I use that gets me the appointment over my competition. After I have prioritized my cards into hot, warm, and soft leads, I prepare for my follow-up emails and videos. I only send personalized emails to my hot and warm leads; my soft prospects receive a generic video (although these have been just as effective—I will explain in a moment).

Now before you start to get butterflies about video, DON'T! With technologies like the smart phone and YouTube, it's relatively simple to send a personalized video. Let me show you how!

- I use my smart phone to create 30-second introductions, and I am very specific with my information and request. It will say something like this:

Hot and warm leads:

"Hi, Mary, it's Jayne Rios with Express Yourself eLearning. I enjoyed connecting with you last night at the PSA event. I know you just returned from vacation and you are probably playing catch-up right now. However, I also know, based on our conversation last night, you need a solid marketing program. I would like to schedule an appointment to see how I could help take some of those tasks off your plate. I will follow-up with you tomorrow to see when it is most convenient for you to meet. Again, I thoroughly enjoyed visiting with you and I look forward to connecting again soon! Talk to you tomorrow and have a great day."

Following-up with video does two things:

1. Out of all the people they met during the event, you will be remembered.
2. It personalizes the experience and sets you apart from your competition.

Soft leads video:

These contacts are not immediate prospects, but they could go from soft to hot with a future career change. The video to your soft contacts is more generic but has the same effect. A generic video simply means you won't use their name or specifics about their company or conversations you had during the event. You want to keep in touch with these people, but you know there isn't a lot of synergy between your two companies. (But always remember everyone knows someone who needs your services!) On my generic videos, I say something like this:

"I was so delighted to visit with you last night at the PSA event. The speaker was incredible, and I learned so much. I am sure you met many people last night, so instead of sending a generic email I thought I would send you a video so you could put a face with a name. If you ever need video or marketing services or know of someone who does, please do me a favor and send them our way. If there is ever anything I can do to be of service to you, please don't hesitate to call. Have a great day, and I hope to see you again in the near future."

After each of my events I will usually create 10 to 15 videos, which takes me around 20 minutes to complete. After creating the videos, I upload them to YouTube, embed them into my emails, hit send, and schedule follow-up calls with my hot and warm prospects.

STEP 4:

Phone call follow-ups are critical. If you tell a prospect that you are going to call the next day, CALL THE NEXT DAY! Integrity and credibility are so important. Do what you say you are going to do. Once you have sent your video, schedule call backs on your calendar with your hot and warm prospects for the day you told them you would. If it's on your calendar, you are more likely to follow up in a timely matter. Don't let distractions keep you from building your business. This is the highest priority the day after the videos are sent, so treat it as such and watch your business grow. When calling the next day, reiterate what you said in the video. Remind them about the personal conversation you had during the event and then ask if they received your video. It's a great conversation starter. Most of my contacts will mention my video before I do—that's how powerful it is.

BONUS:

Another secret weapon of mine is to send a PERSONALIZED thank you note to my hot prospects. Once I complete my video, I write a quick thank you note and send it through the mail. Again, I am setting myself and my company apart from my competition by personalizing my communications.

So how has this process of following up after networking events helped grow my company? IT BUILT MY COMPANY! In 2004, I started my company and worked from home, juggling an expanding workload and a two-year-old. A year later, my husband and I welcomed our second child, and my priority remained the same: spending quality time with my children. To grow my company from home, I began by networking online, using social media, and sending videos. As my company grew, so did my children. Once they started school, I began attending live networking events and using the above plan. Within one year, I had built my company to high six figures, with an office and employees. However, even to this day I schedule my day around school. When my children return home, I am there. I can testify that this **Increasing Sales After the Networking Event with Video** process works. By using video, you will build relationships faster, secure appointments easier, and stay miles ahead of your competition.

Contact Jayne Rios to learn more about Monetizing Your Message with video and eCourses at 855-456-9876 or www.expressyourselfelearning.com

ALICE HEIMAN

Alice Heiman makes a profound difference in how people approach networking, lead generation, and sales. A consummate networker, both online and off, Alice has authored the ebook *Connecting Your Way to New Business*, created The BizTalk Blender®, and offers training on topics like generating leads without cold calling, handling objections, and closing the deal and social selling.

Website: www.aliceheiman.com

YouTube: http://www.youtube.com/user/AliceHeiman

Facebook: https://www.facebook.com/aliceheiman

Twitter: https://twitter.com/aliceheiman

Google+:   https://plus.google.com/u/0/113830723963084738905/
posts?partnerid=gplp0

LinkedIn: http://www.linkedin.com/in/aliceheiman

CHAPTER 11
NETWORKING: JUST SHOWING UP DOESN'T CUT IT!

by Alice Heiman

Do you network effectively in a crowd? Does the time and money you spend attending professional association meetings, trade shows, and networking events turn into revenue?

As business professionals, whether we are charged with selling or not, building a strong, usable network is critical. It is one of the most valuable assets you have today and, built correctly, your network can be leveraged when you need resources, funding, employees, and new customers.

Attending the right events is one of the easiest ways to build your network and generate leads. But just showing up, doesn't cut it.

Frequently I walk into "networking" events and see the following: People register, walk into the meeting room, find their friends or co-workers, and start chatting, ignoring all the wonderful people around them they could be meeting.

That's not networking.

So here is the way to make the most of the events you attend. Make a plan. Don't just show up at the event. Start by setting some goals for the event, schedule time on your calendar to do the follow-up, and plan to arrive early, possibly even volunteer to help greet. Find other early arrivers and start a conversation. It's sometimes easier to get started when there are fewer people in the room.

Here are 10 things you can do to ensure that the time and money you spend networking strengthen your network:

1. Figure out the best places to meet the people you need to know. Many make the mistake of networking only to find prospects. I advise looking for people you can do business with, collaborate with and develop into a referral source. Notice I didn't say sell to. Yes, you may meet a prospect at an event but you are not there to sell. You are there to develop relationships. These relationships can turn into something much more valuable than one sale. So make sure you are networking in places where you can meet all of the types of people you need in your network. If you are only looking for your next sale, you might miss a valuable relationship.

   Here are a few organizations to consider:

   - American Marketing Association (AMA)
   - American Business Women's Association (ABWA)
   - American Institute of CPAs
   - Builders Association
   - Commercial Real Estate Women (CREW)
   - eWomen Network
   - Chambers of Commerce
   - Human Resource Associations (SHRM)
   - Society of Women Engineers (SWE)
   - The Network for Women in Business
   - National Association of Insurance and Financial Advisors (NAIFA)
   - Lions, Rotary, Zonta, and Soroptimists service clubs
   - Realtors Association

   There are many wonderful business and service organizations for almost any profession you may be in. Don't just attend your professional organization; visit others as well. The people who attend these are potential clients, collaborators, and referral sources.

2. Set goals for each networking event. My first goal is to schedule time to do the follow-up work that makes the event a success for me. What good is it to start to develop a relationship and not continue to build it? Set a goal to meet at least five new people and do follow-up meetings

with at least three. You might have a goal to meet the president of the organization or a specific member. Set your goals before you go and hold yourself accountable.

3. Dress for success. Wear something comfortable that makes you feel like a million bucks. A nice logo shirt with nice slacks or a skirt is appropriate most of the time. A dress or suit might be appropriate for some events. Don't overlook this important detail. Always wear your company name tag. If you look great, you will feel great and be more comfortable meeting new people. Ladies, you might want to wear something with pockets so you can keep your business cards and a pen handy. You don't want to waste valuable time digging in your purse.

4. Attend new events with a member who will introduce you. If you don't know any members, call the organizer and ask to attend as someone's guest. Call that person in advance and get acquainted so they can do a good job introducing you. If there is someone specific you want an introduction to, let them know so they can make it happen.

5. Make it a point to meet the people you don't know. Don't just talk with your friends and coworkers. Say "hi" and keep moving. Bringing a guest is a good excuse to work the room. Be sure to introduce them to as many people as possible without rushing. If you are finding it hard to break away from those you know, say something like, "I don't mean to rush off, but I want to introduce my guest to a few more people" or "Great talking to you, there are a few other people I need to say hi to. Enjoy the event."

6. Have plenty of business cards with you. Should I have to mention this? The answer is, yes. I can't tell you how many times I've been at events and asked someone for their card and can't believe my ears when they say, "I didn't bring any" or "I am out." Always have plenty of cards handy. Keep extras in your car, briefcase, purse, pockets, and anywhere else you can think of. Have a pen handy to write notes on the cards as you collect them. It helps you remember later when you want to schedule a follow-up.

7. Make conversation by asking questions. Don't pitch your business. Don't even mention your business unless you are asked. Ask good questions and listen. Find something you have in common.

If you are shy or not sure how to start a conversation, you can always ask some of the following questions to get you started.

- "How long have you been a member? What are some of the benefits you enjoy?"
- "Tell me about your business. What do you enjoy most about it?"
- "Are you from this area?"
- "It is my first time at this event and I don't know anyone. Would you save me by talking to me?"

8. Be prepared with a great answer to "What do you do?" If asked, give your 30-second answer. Then share briefly the results your customers receive, in the form of a short success story. Rehearse—not so that it sounds scripted, but so that it sounds great. Stating the name of your company and your title is not enough. You need to say something that helps people understand what you do and engage them.

Instead of "Hi, I am Ben, I'm a business banker from ABC Bank" say something like, "Hi, I am Ben from ABC Bank. I make it easy for small businesses to do their banking." If asked how you do that, share a story.

Here is an example of a short success story:

"I recently worked with a company that had a great product, but couldn't close the sales needed to make a profit. After interviewing their salespeople, I put together a training that delivered the skills they needed. Within three weeks their sales increased by 20%."

9. Ask for the type of business you want and be specific. At the end of your success story, if you still have a captive audience, be sure to tell them the type of business you are looking for. How do you do that without seeming salesy? By asking them first, "So tell me, what kind of business are you looking for?" Once they answer you can say, "I'll keep that in mind, and I am looking for . . ."

Here's an example:

"I am looking for small to mid-size companies that want to increase their sales and have a budget for sales training. If you know the CEOs of any companies like that, I would love the opportunity to meet with them and learn about what they are trying to accomplish to see if I can be of service."

If they have referrals for you right there, be prepared to write them down and ask if they would feel comfortable introducing you.

10. Follow up. You'll have plenty of time to do this because the time needed will be scheduled on your calendar. Networking is useless if you don't do any follow-up. After the event, immediately enter the business cards you collected into your database. Be sure to add any notes you made on the cards during the event. I always add the name and date of the event so I remember where we met. If I send an email or a card to follow up, I make a note of that also. Be sure to connect on LinkedIn and other appropriate social media. Make sure to schedule meetings with those who have the potential to be customers, collaborators, and referral sources.

Develop a networking strategy. Be clear on your goals and choose the events you attend carefully. Follow the 10 steps above to turn all the time, money, and effort spent at networking events into a strong, usable network you can leverage.

DR. GENEVIEVE KUMAPLEY

Genevieve Kumapley, PharmD is the Founder and the Executive Director of MyGOAL Inc., a 501 c (3) non-profit Autism organization and Haven International. Dr. Kumapley has a Doctor of Pharmacy Degree and practices as a Board Certified Oncology Pharmacist. She is a recipient of several leadership awards including the 2013 Role Model Award from NAACP. She has been featured on several TV and Radio networks including ABC News. She is married to Robert and they have 3 children.

Website: www.mygoalautism.org

Facebook: www.facebook.com/genevieve.kumapley

Facebook: www.facebook.com/mygoalautism

Facebook: www.facebook.com/autismafrica

Twitter: www.twitter.com/gkumapley

Twitter: www.twitter.com/mygoalautism

Linkedin: www.linkedin.com/in/genevieve kumapley

Youtube: www.youtube.com/mygoalautism

CHAPTER 12
NO PASSION, NO GAIN
by Dr. Genevieve Kumapley

P- Perception that fuels the push

A- Assessment of the environment

S- Share Your Story

S Support (Support System)

I- Interest of the people for Insights

O- Organization

N- Network

Your network to your net worth is not defined by material accumulation but the impact you are able to make. Primarily, making an impact is driven by PASSION. This is the fuel that provides the drive to push through diverse circumstances and yield great outcomes; which make a difference in people's lives.

As I evaluate the strategies that have not only brought me success, but also access to opportunities that were created through networking, I resolve that it was the net effect of *passion.* Passion resonates through the 7 principles of Perception, Assessment of the environment, the Sharing of the Story, gaining the Support, determining the Interest of the people for insight, the need for Organizational skills to sustain the effect of the connection and the capacity to capitalize and expand one's Network.

In 2006, when I thought of starting a project related to my son's condition, I didn't quite know how I was going to make it happen. As I waited patiently in the doctor's lounge for my son to finish his therapy appointment, I began to put my thoughts on paper. I had conceived the vision and mission of an

Autism organization that would eventually be birthed in 2008. My next step was to ask a friend to create a logo, which he did; but I filed it for later use. Interestingly, I did not take the project seriously at that time.

Two years later, I began to feel this burning desire to learn more about myself and get closer to God. This "push" led me to speak with individuals from a spiritual perspective which eventually led to my enrollment into a Bible School. History Maker's Bible school was very untraditional; it challenged the students to draw on our desires and passions to make a difference in the world. When confronted with the opportunity and challenge, I decided to revisit the idea I had in 2006 and developed a plan that I began to implement it. I shared the idea with key supporters who directed, encouraged and coached me to start the 501 c (3) non-profit organization dedicated to supporting families affected by Autism.

The 7 key lessons and strategies that influenced my ability to utilize my network and to effectively achieve success are as follows:

Perception- There was a burning desire in me to make a difference in the lives of individuals with Autism. Generally, I am driven to volunteerism and help people whenever I get an opportunity to do so. As an individual who is highly energized, finding a project and program to which I could dedicate my time and talent was critical. Once I found it, it was very easy to make an impact. I discovered that perception of what matters and is valuable to you will enable you to rise above disappointments or situations where/when people do not readily respond to you.

Assessment- I assessed the value of sharing my experiences and whenever I had the opportunity to share my story, I did! Many of us jump into different projects without really taking time to assess why we are involved. Sometimes we are fearful of doing something new or different because we fail to invest necessary time and comprehensive planning. Detailed planning helps eliminate fear of the unknown. I read books on starting a non-profit, and I spoke to individuals who had successfully started one. It is also important to examine the climate within your desired organization or cause and your competitors. This knowledge shapes how you dialogue and 'sell' your vision and product. If there are redundancies in what you are doing, you might be blindsided and miss the opportunity to engage in something else that might be impactful. As I reached the 5 year mark, I engaged my Board in a dialogue about strategic planning for the future. Hard questions were asked, and where there was need, professional strategists were engaged to help us line up our vision to the changing environment we're serving.

Share your story and your vision. I shared my story about the challenges I had finding information to help my son and why my organization could help close the gap. I shared the vision with anyone and everyone I met and was amazed that I raised supporters and obtained the coveted 501 c (3) IRS status in the span of in the span of 6 weeks (whereas it may normally take years to achieve this). I was initially reluctant to share my story, but over time I discovered that people are interested in you as a person, including the reason you believe in something and your value system. Similar to the for-profit leader, the non-profit leader must be willing to express, explain, and wine and dine people, in an effort to share the worth of their vision. One's vision can only be revealed through vulnerability and open and candid conversation. This also affords an opportunity for dialogue which could result in potential partnerships.

Gain *Supporters.* Sharing the story led to gaining some key supporters. My immediate network, family, church, co-workers, strangers, neighbors joined me in launching several successful fundraising campaigns. Over the years, this network has expanded to developing specific key partners. Often times we limit our support base to those within our circles. It is imperative to identify the different levels of your supporters. The base supporters are those key individuals you can call on at critical moments. These may be your high level individuals to whom you will reach out for expert advice etc. They are the ACE's in your deck of supporters. Use that card sparingly. You also need supporters who are encouragers and who believe in what you are doing. You can draw on them for consistent refueling. These individuals are your cheerleaders during times of exhaustion and frustration. Cheerleaders will support you even if things are not going great. Keep in mind they don't always come in the form of a family member. Another group of supporters are people who are around for a season or for their own personal reason. Understand that they are looking for something in return for helping you. You should support their vision and expect them to support yours. The caveat is that a time will come when this type of relationship will lose its value. Learn to identify that early on, cut your losses and move on. When I first started, I didn't understand these different types of support systems. So I pulled the ACE's at the wrong time, they got frustrated and I became too sensitive and hurt that some people I expected to stick around were "bailing out" on me. As the years passed, I have now learned what category each of my supporters fits in and this process enables me to effectively leverage and manage my relationships.

Determine the *Interest of the people for Insights.* I learned on this journey that it is important to know and understand what the constituents are interested in. Conducting focus groups and getting feedback is critical in being relevant. As a non-profit or community based organization leader, I found that it was important to be aware of what projects funders are interested in funding. I once learned that a funder was interested in doing some work in Africa and Autism. I called him and asked for an opportunity to speak with him. The most important lesson is to learn something about the person you are meeting. In other words, research them, to ascertain important information such as their likes and dislikes and their funding history. Armed with this type of information, I went to visit this potential funder. I didn't ask for anything outright. The funder however, was impressed with the vision for what I wanted to do in Africa. What I lacked in experience, I gained in passion. He commented that he saw someone who was passionate to get things done and he was willing to invest and take a chance to fund the project.

Organization is also a key factor. Setting up a strong organizational structure is necessary in establishing a solid foundation. This is because growth will likely occur as you begin to share your story and gain supporters. Hence, without the key structures in place, your ability to expand and grow will be limited. Identify key individuals with certain backgrounds (especially, the board composition) who can provide the key structural components you will need and specifically seek to draw those individuals out in your network.

Network, Network, Network. Every interaction with any person is an open door to networking. The ultimate goal in expansion and capacity building is all about widening the network to which you are connected. One thing I know for sure is that key partnerships and collaborations came from doing the 6 steps above within the network of people to which I was exposed. This ranges from individuals in the communities I serve, to programs in which I participated. A valuable tool to increasing my capacity has been attaining skill sets that enable me to grow personally and professionally. I attend conferences, training programs and seminars in order to learn the tools of the trade. Interestingly, attending these conferences and training seminars has opened great doors and opportunities for me to demonstrate what I care about as well as gain key supporters to expand the business.

The net gain in networking is maximized when you are motivated and passionate about what you are doing. This must be clearly reflected in your day-to-day interaction with people. Where there is no passion there is no gain.

WENDI CAPLAN-CARROLL

Wendi Caplan-Carroll is currently Constant Contact's area director for the northeast. She has more than 20 years of experience in sales management, marketing, promotion, executive coaching, and facilitation. She has educated more than 30,000 small businesses on behalf of Constant Contact.

Prior to Constant Contact, Wendi ran her own coaching firm. She spent more than 15 years in sales and marketing at major broadcast companies. She's a certified executive coach, DISC analyst, and creative facilitator.

CHAPTER 13
Y IS FOR YENTA: LESSONS ON HOW BEING CURIOUS CAN HELP YOU TO FULFILL YOUR DREAMS

by Wendi Caplan-Carroll

One of my favorite Yiddish words is Yenta. According to Dictionary.com, *"a Yenta is a person, especially a woman, who is a busy body or gossip."* You may remember Yenta the matchmaker in *Fiddler on the Roof*. That character was portrayed as well intentioned, but most definitely pushy. To me a Yenta is one who thrives on making connections and building relationships both on- and offline. My own Yenta-ness (so to speak) is not so much about gossiping as much as it is about my own curiosity. My interest in people and their stories has always made it very easy for me to connect with them. Quite frankly, I've always been a natural networker. The Yenta in me has helped me make friends and score jobs, projects, friendships, and apartments. It's even enabled me to connect others to opportunities as well.

Some helpful Yenta tips that helped me and can also help you:

Be nosy: Yes, I said it, "Be nosy." The best Yentas are curious. They want to know it all. That curiosity will guide you to deeper conversations with people. What I mean is to be really interested in learning about someone. Ask questions and then listen away. Always ask open-ended questions. No yes/no answers allowed when having a conversation. Make people talk. Learn what makes them tick, and then try to connect with that. Always let your curiosity drive the questioning. Don't have an agenda. Let the conversation be your guide.

Be real: These days, everyone is telling you to be authentic. That's because people can see right through phony. The more real you are during your in-person networking as well as your networking online, the more people will get to know your awesomeness and will want to help you.

Be open: Be open to meeting new people and experiencing new activities. Don't be afraid to step into a conversation, and make it a point to reach out to someone new each and every day. Be open to the possibilities of where new relationships can lead you and to meeting different types of people.

Be honest: Always be honest about yourself, what you can do, and even what you can't do. Being honest "frees" you in a great respect. This freedom allows for much more forward action to happen. It's kind of like letting go of something that isn't good for you. Being honest in networking will open you up to those special moments that can often lead you to the right opportunity.

Be lovable or at least likeable: No one wants to help out a "schmuck". Truly. You want to be the person that people want to be around! A big part of networking is not only about you reaching out to people, but also about people reaching out to you. Be likeable by listening and giving more than you are talking and asking of others. People will appreciate you and will actually want to get to know you more when you are not always talking and pushing yourselves on to them. Show you care! It's much more appealing.

Be ready to make a match: Be perceived as the connector. When meeting, don't just think about what you can do for them, but begin to think about how others you know can benefit them as well. Being able to make those connections truly makes you an invaluable and unforgettable resource. Be ready to make that match!

Be hungry: A good Yenta is always watching his or her figure, but also recognizes that having a hunger for opportunity is critical to success. Always crave connection, growth, and increased engagement with others. Don't be afraid to have a big appetite for this!

Be bold (Fake it if you have to): Even if you are painfully shy, in order to be really good at networking you need to step out of your comfort zone. There are times when even I, the ultimate "Yenta", walk into a room and get nervous (like every time!). I learned a very important lesson years ago from an awesome boss of mine. She was probably one of the smartest and most dynamic people I had ever worked with. She admitted to me that every single morning she would look at herself in the mirror and think, "When will they realize that I have no idea what I'm doing?" The truth is that we all get nervous. It's a fact that it is human nature to be nervous! Learn to walk into a new situation with your head held high. Own it!

Don't be desperate: Walking into any situation feeling sorry for yourself is not the way to meet anyone or find the right opportunities. I remember a particularly stressful period when I was at a crossroads in life. I set up shop as an executive coach and had planned to rock my business with a ton of clients. Unfortunately, that wasn't to be. I now know why. I didn't really *want* a solo coaching practice. At the time, it sounded good, but in reality it ended up draining me. When I was out networking at events and with colleagues (this was well before Facebook and Twitter), I rarely landed a new client. I was really insecure about my abilities, and my 30-second elevator pitch made no sense even to me. I probably came across as desperate and certainly not passionate about my business. Once I realized what I wanted to do (a full-time job with a company dedicated to small businesses), my networks opened up and I found the perfect opportunity for me. Coincidence? I don't think so! A good Yenta is confident, and when she realizes something isn't right, she walks away from it and focuses on what is right.

With all the new channels now available to us to grow our networks online via the many social channels, it's truly a Yenta networking paradise. Online social networking carries many of the same rules as above. Some important things to remember about social networking:

Social networking is not about selling: It's just another channel to build relationships. People fail when they view social networks as a place to push sales messages or brag about themselves. Social networks are to be used for you to share who you are and how you help others.

It's about quality, not quantity: I'm a firm believer that the quality of your connections is more important than the quantity. Of course we all want to grow our followings online, but pay more attention to *how* you can engage with those you are connecting with. Too large a social network might be tough to manage. Take your time building your network. Connections and relationships take time to build and grow.

A true Yenta knows that networking is not all about her (or him - yes, there is many a male Yenta): Don't overshare, or over speak. Make sure to listen. You'll learn so much about them and be able to provide them with what they need, not what you think they do.

Applying my Yenta rules truly has opened up so many opportunities for me and I embrace them all every single day. We all have the Yenta inside of us. Don't be afraid to let it shine. It can truly turn a dream you have into a reality.

A few years ago I was in the process of adopting my daughter. It was a never-ending wait that went from 12 months to suddenly 36-plus months. It seemed as if my hopes for becoming a mother were not to be. A former co-worker of mine grabbed me for a cup of coffee one day and said to me, "Wendi, you are already a mother. You must keep that goal in your mind and be determined that by the end of this year you will get your referral." It was a hard thing to believe as the country that I was adopting from had literally almost halted adoptions. But, I thought, it can't hurt. I tapped into my inner Yenta and just let it guide me. I immersed myself in the adoption world. I decided to become the person that other waiting families could come to for help and support. I connected with adoption specialists. I blogged from my heart. I created events for the community. I became very well known by my agency because of all these activities. One day out of the blue they called me and asked me if I would be willing to pioneer another program in another country. No promises, they said, but why not? Two months later I got my referral and Lia-Rose was home nine months later.

If I hadn't been so visible or so helpful to others, I truly believe the agency would never have asked us to be part of the program. This just proves that following the Yenta rules for networking can lead you down a path of success in both your personal and professional lives. So remember to be bold, be visible, be helpful, be you—and great things will happen!

JESELLE ELI

Jeselle Eli has committed her life to teaching people how to radically change their lives by helping them tap into their own potential in order to live the life of their dreams. Through her own journey of trials, tribulations, successes, and triumphs, Jeselle has learned first-hand through work with her own coaches the power of an objective perspective in life. She works with individuals, couples, families, and companies to transform the way they understand themselves and others.

Website: www.jeselleeli.com

Facebook: www.facebook.com/JeselleEli

Twitter: www.twitter.com/JustJeselle

LinkedIn: www.linkedin.com/JeselleEli

YouTube: www.youtube.com/JeselleTV

CHAPTER 14

THE ART OF DELIBERATE NETWORKING

by Jeselle Eli

Networking. For some people it scares the daylights out of them. For others, it is the life blood of their existence. I am one of the latter. I am ridiculously thrilled by networking. And keep in mind, my ability to network was not always up to par, let alone existent for that matter.

I would like to start by answering a question that I wish someone had taught me when I was still in grade school: Why is networking so important?

Networking is important because, first and foremost, not much is done alone. With a team, everything can be smoother, easier, bigger, better, and a congratulatory journey on the way to whatever awesome venture you and your newfound mates are working toward. Networking allows people to intertwine in a web of mysterious and magical meetings, whereby one hand washes the other in ways you could not even fathom. I am a big believer, supporter, participant, and teacher in the laws of the universe, and I know that each of us is just handshakes and hugs away from the person you probably thought was impossible to meet. So let's dive in to some networking principles.

The Law of Attraction in Networking

The Law of Attraction states that which is like unto itself is drawn. The phrases birds of a feather flock together, or he and I were cut from the same cloth, or the apple didn't fall too far from the tree are all in alignment with the laws of the universe. In regards to networking, I want to cut straight though the meat and potatoes of it all.

I assume you are already in business and continuously in a strategy thought process of how to achieve your company's next step or what needs to happen in order for the projections of the quarter to be reached. I can guarantee that there are people in the equation who may not be there yet who can help, assist or facilitate a smoother result or, even better, an amazing partnership for the future. When we look at net worth, it is - like life - not an event, but a journey. With that said, I challenge you to consider that every single person you meet is part of your team—from the teller at the bank to the person whose sneeze you blessed on the train, the person who forgot their glasses on the counter before you at the hotel, and the person with whom you just shared a very energetically driven smile in passing on your way to a meeting. Does this sound a bit weird to you? I'm sure it does. Well, when looking to do awesome and extraordinary things in this life, when it's weird, it's working!

Let me share a story with you. I was at the gym recently, and there were two people there together, chatting away. I was no part of their conversation, but I found my way in—simply and subtly, with no intention but to say hello as I was busy getting my daily cardio in. The young lady mentioned that she had left her bag at the airport, and I said "You left your bag at the airport?" Being a person who is in and out of airports regularly, I was genuinely interested in what had happened to this lady's belongings. We all got to talking while we were working out, learning about their travel troubles. I then came to find out that the gentleman was from Philadelphia (a small detail I forgot to mention: I was in a small gym in Lusaka, Zambia on the other side of the world, and I was having a random tri-state area connection.) As our conversation furthered, I found out that this young man was the grandson of Sylvia—THE Sylvia of Sylvia's Soul Food Restaurant in Harlem. I had been looking into opening a restaurant in Zambia or producing some cooking products to bring to the food industry. I was immediately like, "Dude…How are we going to bring some of Sylvia's products to Africa? We need to share some soul food with the motherland."

This example is just one of too-many-to-count meetings with people who know people who know people. Eventually you get really good at manifesting who you want to meet, and then you just—boom—go straight to the players themselves.

This leads me to my first power point in networking:

The Power of Intention

Networking goes beyond working the room and meeting everyone. After all, what are you really going to do if you collect 100 cards at an event with 3,000 people? I am sure your ambitious side is telling you that you are going to email all of them one by one and greet them on your fantastic meeting. Sure, okay. Really! I do believe you. But let's say that you do not get around to doing that. How about we make your networking experience more fun and rewarding and intentional? The power of intention—and, even better, deliberate intention—is all about seeking out that person you are looking for. A secret of the universe is that whatever you want, wants you as well. So chances are that if your intentions are clearly defined as to who you want to meet, in order to do what, and how you can enrich each other, the universe will plant in your path a person or a few that will help elevate your dreams, desires, plans, and projects to places you didn't see coming. An intention can be as vague as "It is my intention to meet someone who will honor and support my dreams fully in a meaningful new friendship." Or it can be up a notch to "It is my intention to meet someone who will play a part in investing or connecting me to the investors necessary to make xyz project happen." Or up a notch even more: "It is my intention to meet Russell Simmons so we can collaborate and plan a meditation hip hop summit retreat."

Whatever—or, better yet, whomever—you want to meet is waiting to meet you too. Depending on the circumstances, trust that the universe is holding your intentions for you and making a way.

Where to Find the People

When you are deliberate with your intentions, you can start to network more strategically. You can go straight to the place where the people are whom you are looking to meet once you identify whom it is you want to meet. For example, let's say you are ready for a serious relationship and you have your soul mate description understood clearly in your mind or on paper; something to consider is where would this person be? Where would they be hanging out? Who could their friends be? Where do I need to show up in order to cross paths and meet this unknown person? The same goes for known people. I wanted to meet Les Brown. His work has been inspiring to me, and he is a mentor for me in my industry. I knew where he was going to be, and I showed up. It was a two-hour flight across country, but because of my deliberate intent, we met and spent quality time together chatting, laughing, and growing a beautiful mutually beneficial relationship between myself and his family. Because of stepping out on faith, intention, and purpose, what I wanted happened—even more exponentially than expected.

Some places that you can find the people you might be looking for to increase your net worth:

- Hotel lobbies, bars, and lounges
- Airports
- Coffee shops and bistros near executive offices
- Shopping or strolling in the happening retailer or market
- At your nearest or not so nearest event

Be a Connector

Don't be stingy! Of course we all meet a range of amazing people all the time. When appropriate, connect the people you know whom you feel can be of direct relational benefit to each other beyond you. The same way you circulate money and give and receive and spend and invest and save, etc., you can do this with your rolodex.

People need people. In the health and wellness seminars I teach, I always say that the difference between illness and wellness is "I" and "We." This holds true in any area of life you wish to focus on or that is important to you.

Now that You've Got the Digits...

Remember: Depending on the circumstances, the network you are looking to build might be a one-night stand or a long-term committed relationship. With those long-term commitments, remember to pace yourself, enjoy the courting period, and really learn to dance the dance with the relationship and let the pieces come together as it will. Patience pays, and I guarantee you that you will enjoy the patience as you begin to master your networking.

Last but not least, the phrase you have probably heard all too often and might forget all too often: Add value! Always add value to any relationship you are building. Value is reciprocal and new network relationships can be so much fun and a blast to experience when you already feel all the value in the boat for all parties.

Set up the party so everyone can win. Set up the party so you can all have fun. And set up the party so everyone feels supported, connected, and benefited for the duration of the dance!

VALERIE C. WELLS

Valerie C. Wells, an information technology, intellectual property, contracts, and federal acquisitions attorney, has led all phases of drafting, negotiating and reviewing complex agreements for high-profile clients such as Navy Pier, a premier Illinois tourist attraction, McCormick Place Convention Center, the largest convention center in North America, and the Smithsonian Institution, the world's largest museum and research complex. Valerie is also passionate about assisting small business owners with growing and developing their businesses. She has counseled small businesses on financial opportunities, including doing business with the federal government. Valerie resides in the DC area.

Email: ValerieCWells@outlook.com

Facebook: www.facebook.com/ValerieCWells

LinkedIn: www.linkedin.com/in/ValerieCWells

CHAPTER 15
I USED TO HATE NETWORKING, BUT NOT ANYMORE!

by Valerie C. Wells

You miss 100% of the shots that you don't take. Ordinarily I would run at warp speed in the opposite direction of a sports analogy, but that analogy was so simple that I intuitively understood it without an explanation. I simply "got it."

Unfortunately, I cannot say the same about networking. I don't get it. Furthermore, I didn't want to. I would rather have the hair on my head waxed one strand at a time (and I have many strands of hair), than engage in any activity that remotely includes or resembles networking. Why the angst? Childhood trauma? No. A bad networking experience? Nope. Not really—at least not one that I wasn't responsible for. Then why have such a severe reaction?

Well, the truth is simple. Networking has never come easily to me. In fact I can admit without reservation that networking is so not my special talent. I just don't want to network. I'd rather read a book. Now don't get me wrong. Intellectually, I understand the concept, but I struggle with the execution.

I have read more networking books than I can recall. I have amassed more one-sentence networking tips than I am tall. Still, at the end of the day, when it comes down to mixing and mingling, if I have to say more than my name, my mind goes blank, my tongue morphs into a double knot, and I head for the nearest corner—and then to the nearest exit. When I am outside and walking away, all kinds of clever repartee floods my head. My mind is a cacophony of witty remarks, thought-provoking questions, and scintillating, but strategic conversation. In fact, I am really very clever. Fuming, I pose the central question of "why"? Why can't I be as clever in a networking setting as I am when I am by myself? Why should I put myself in networking situations anyway? What is the point?

Then a single truth makes the gut-check rounds in my head. I am not a silo. I cannot accomplish the things that I would like to accomplish by myself. Succeeding means interacting with people—and not always in a work setting where you know your colleagues or in a social setting with your friends. Sometimes it means "talking to" and "interacting with" people you don't know.

To this day I still cannot understand how I can drive multi-million-dollar transactions but struggle with "chit-chat" and "getting to know you" situations, especially since my success at work depends on an ability to skillfully interact, build relationships, and—yes, you guessed it—network. In fact, I have observed that, if I need to network for my job, I can instantly flip a switch in my head, transform into an alter ego named "Holly Hostess," and network with a capital N. I can not only survive, but also excel in that context. Yet when it comes to using those same skills for myself in a networking scenario, I could flip the freaking switch all day long for one week straight with no results and no explanation for the disconnect between my brain and my mouth. What is the problem?

That question might never really be answered. In fact, I have come to understand that spending time berating myself is damaging and a waste. More importantly, it obscures larger truths about myself. The larger truth is that my life's path has always been "non-traditional." Consequently, it was always pointless for me to think that I could network in a traditional manner with any degree of ease. I had to define networking for myself and then approach it in a manner more conducive to my soul. Ever since I recognized, honored, and made peace with that fact, I have been able to spin the concept of networking in a way that fits my "unique self."

So what works for me?

If I had to put a name to it, I would call it "opportunity networking." No, not networking with people to cultivate opportunities, but rather networking by recognizing and embracing opportunities as they come my way. It is my way of flipping the script. When networking for myself, talking to people I don't know might scare me; on the other hand, to me, opportunities are adventures waiting to happen. So rather than dwelling on making small talk with people I don't know (which would quickly send me into my own version of networking hell), I focus on the opportunity or adventure and find that I can talk with the people who accompany the opportunities.

The shift in emphasis might seem negligible, but it has made a world of difference in the way that I perceive and approach networking. Creating and pursuing opportunities related to my personal interests, even in a network setting, is exciting. That focus simply works. What also works for me is the fact that networking is not always about sitting in a room with people you don't know and making small talk. It's not always about how well you network or how many business cards you collect. The internet and social media make it possible to connect people and ideas across time zones and continents.

Today I've used my smartphone to sign a petition with 209,000 signatures from around the world. I've used my laptop to email my online course tutor who lives in Malaysia. I've powered up my tablet and called friends who were poolside eating nachos at a resort in Mexico. My LinkedIn contacts connect me to millions of professionals. I use apps like Facebook and Skype to keep up with my family and friends whenever I leave the country. I found both my husband and my last job on the internet. And I didn't have to leave my chair. We have taken the roughly 126,000,000,000 acres comprising the planet Earth and reduced them down to the size of a 15-inch monitor. *If networking is the art of cultivating people, then technology has become the heart of the art,* offering everyone the opportunity to develop an enormous pool of local, national, and international contacts in a relatively short period of time.

In short, by changing my focus and using non-traditional means, I can network in ways that resonate with me.

What works for you? It might help to consider the following:

1. **"You miss 100% of the shots that you don't take." –Wayne Gretzky**

It's true. You really do miss all of the shots that you don't take. You were never meant to sit on the sidelines. This is true in life and is equally true when networking. Discover what works for you, and then do what works for you. Take the shot.

2. "You are not a twin." –Ruby L. Davis

I received that startling bit of information when I was whining for the 75th time about attending a networking event by myself later that evening. After spending hours getting dressed, I'd decided to stay home rather than go alone. My mother had been quietly watching my theatrics and, right before I turned around to go back upstairs, she called my name, looked me straight in the eye, and simply said "You are not a twin." She went on to say that I came here by myself, I'd most likely leave here by myself, and I'd be going out of her door and attending that networking event by myself. I listened to my mother, gathered my courage, and went to the event. Once there, I managed to meet one or two people who made the evening enjoyable. More importantly, I was proud of my mother for reminding me of the woman she'd raised me to be, and I was proud of myself for listening and remembering. By the way, my mother's message works even if you happen to be a twin. Chances are that you and your twin are not conjoined.

3. "Never let the fear of striking out get in your way." –Babe Ruth

Fear feels real, and the feeling can immobilize you. However, it is just a feeling, and feelings are not necessarily facts. Fear happens when we forget or never realize how powerful and magnificent we truly are. Feel the feeling if you must, but above all else, keep moving forward.

As for me, I'd still rather read a book than network in the traditional sense. I might always feel that way. But there's how I feel, and then there's reality. The truth is, my net worth increased exponentially as I recognized and respected the value of developing business and professional relationships. Another truth is that virtually every interesting opportunity, experience, or adventure that I've ever had has come through networking. Whether teaching corporate law in South Africa, leading the process to select an architect for a new museum on the National Mall, or assisting a financial start-up for the federal government, the common denominator has been networking. The common result: increased value, increased income, increased profits.

So do I really still hate networking in light of those results? Let's just say I have warmed up considerably to the concept and continue to perfect the execution.

GRETA DOUGLAS

Greta A. Douglas is a coach, strategist, and motivational speaker. As the founder of Sankofa Empowering Women's Alliance, she has the privilege of working with women business owners who are struggling to find a balance in their life which may prevent them from building a strong foundation in their business. Working together, they create strategies and solutions which lead to transformational results, a clear vision, and a plan for continued success.

She knows that your health is your wealth and makes time to live a balanced life by connecting with her inner spirit and conversations with God, family, and friends. Greta celebrates more than 8 years in the direct sales industry where her passion for training and coaching was born. As a true believer in multiple streams of income, she has embarked on building her noble enterprise by collaborating with other Chief Empowerment Officers, being a lifetime student, and traveling the world.

Email: Greta@GretaDouglas.com

Facebook: www.facebook.com/Greta Douglas

Twitter: www.twitter.com/GretaDouglas

Websites: www.GretaDouglas.com
www.SEWAlliance.com
www.NWIBBoston.com

CHAPTER 16
SIMPLY YOU

by Greta Douglas

Long gone are the days of just going to networking events where you are collecting business cards and trying to meet most of the people in the room. If you're like I used to be, the rubber band is still on those cards with hopes of making it into the database for follow-up. Nowadays, it's about making connections, building relationships, and simply being you.

There are so many ways to network. It doesn't just have to be at events. Today, networking happens when you learn and share interests with someone else. You never know who is waiting for you to show up and play big, which is why it's never a good idea to sit quiet and wait for someone to walk over to you to ask your name. You must be bold and true to your passion and share it even before any questions are asked.

When networking, try to always connect with the individuals who interest you and are in alignment with your values and goals. Always allow your authentic self to come through. Be genuine in your approach because who's better at being you than you? Trying to be anyone else is second rate and not worth it. It's your time to stand out and show up so the world can share your gifts and talents.

If you ever find yourself in a group where people are introducing themselves, make sure to really listen. Don't sit back and simply think about how you are going to introduce yourself. And definitely don't start comparing what you do to that person. This is a key moment. At this time, you are being given an opportunity to ask questions to explore what this person's interests are and possibly how you can provide a solution for a problem they may have or they may have a solution for a problem that you may have.

It's important to simply be your true and authentic self. It takes way too much time and effort to pretend to be someone else. But don't be confused. It's okay to say that you're an author while you're in the process of writing even though you haven't been published. There are some things that you will have to simply talk into existence and act accordingly. This is being true to your authentic self. You have dreams and aspirations but if you keep them bottled up inside you may never bring them to life.

So what does being your authentic self really mean? It means no holding back, allowing your brilliance and greatness to stand out. It also means you are able to hold your head up high and be proud of the person that you currently are and the one that you're becoming. You have a gift, a talent, a cause to share. So why not be you and just glow about it. You can tell the difference from a person that is passionate or loving what they are offering from a person that is following a script and hoping that you'll listen. One shows confidence and the other seems fake. One sparks your interest and you start to lean in for more and with the other one you may be wondering what you are going to have for lunch. So in all that you do, do it to the best of your ability and be happy about it, because you are there for a reason.

Networking has allowed me to begin living many of my dreams. Let me start by explaining why you are reading this chapter today. I went to a Social Media Boot Camp given by the Network for Women in Business in April 2012. I learned so much about the world of social media and met some very inspiring women. This opportunity allowed me to connect with Toni Coleman-Brown, live and in person. I knew of her through her Facebook Business Page for the Network for Women in Business and also through a direct selling company that we were both involved with at one time. But our true connection began that day. My intention before going to the event was to show up and make this opportunity worthwhile and make sure that I connected with individuals that shared my interests and folks who I could stay connected with. It's amazing how when you have a purposeful intention that aligns with your values and goals how these things show up. Over the course of the year, Toni and I built our friendship to where I am; also one of the Founding Regional Directors and the Regional Director Liaison for the Network for Women in Business. My intent was to be around like-minded women that wanted to build a movement that would uplift, educate and celebrate women business owners. Now, I'm living my dream on purpose.

I started a group a couple of years ago called Boston Builds It Big. This group was brought together to support direct sellers across companies to reach out, network, train, learn and grow with each other. This group is now transitioning into a Strategic Alliance Group that is all about successfully helping others reach the next level in their business. This too started with speaking with other business owners in network marketing to see what they were looking for. Now I'm living yet another dream on purpose.

My organization, Sankofa Empowering Women's Alliance, is the essence of when women get together and focus on the matters that are important for growth in all areas of their life. The Akan word, Sankofa, symbolizes one taking from the past and the wisdom that comes from learning from it. Bringing what's good into the present in order to make positive progress through the use of applied knowledge in order to achieve full potential in building your future. This is not done in a vacuum. This is done by purposefully connecting with others so you can reach success as you define it. This happens by sharing, learning and exposing on a bigger scale. It may take more than a village to build a successful business but it starts with building one relationship and connection at a time.

When your vision becomes clear about why you are attending certain events, sharing your business opportunity, or you're announcing what it is you're doing, it will no longer feel like work. It will just become a part of who you are because you are being truly authentic in your approach, which will allow for your message to be consistent and on point. I'm not saying that it may not change over time. There will be times when your message may change because you are growing, tweaking, and just making your message clearer but the essence of your message will usually be the same because you are being authentic in your delivery.

So how are you being your authentic self? How are you allowing others to know you and the products or services that you represent? If you are looking for ways to allow the true you to step out, contact me to set up your power hour for us to explore the possibilities. I am blessed to do what I love and that is to support women in reaching and defining success on their terms.

If you are ever in the Massachusetts area, please join the Network for Women in Business, Boston, MA Chapter at one of our events. Check out our Events Calendar at www.networkforwomeninbusiness.com for more information.

Remember to be your true and authentic self for life is a journey, so enjoy the ride!

AUDREY REED

Audrey Reed is a highly acclaimed Marriage/Relationship/Life Coach, Entrepreneur Producer, Author and Motivational Speaker. With over 25 years of experience. Audrey is compassionate, she coaches people dealing with issues of life, relationship, and marital problems. As a coach she specializes in helping married couples overcome infidelity.

She recently launched a Charter Club for women called Powerful Women Empowering, which is the launch pad for women entrepreneurs and women between dreams and actuality. Audrey states" Individually we have power, yet collectively we are a power source/resources for all." This is the only Network that you can call your BFF!

Audrey is a devoted wife of 31 years, a loving mother to three adult children, and a dedicated "Glam'Ma to three grandchildren.

She can be reached @

Ok2LoveAgain.com

PowerfulWomenEmpowering.com

ThatsAudrey.com

CHAPTER 17

WORK THE NET AND DON'T GET CAUGHT IN IT!

by Audrey Reed

Work the Net!

Networking is about two things: information and people—and how you can connect them to create powerful partnerships. The people who are your potential customers want information. This is why information is the new currency. So let's get the money flowing and get the information out there online. Let's work the Net!

The Net can be your power source. It is definitely one of your best resources today. Try to think of it as a place where you can receive multiple streams of income. So don't just stick with one idea to network, work it all. Google everything and anything in order to find the place where the people who need your information reside. The Net can feed you, teach you, and equip you. It is a powerful transporter of your dreams; use it to draw your ideal customers to your online hub and you will see success and your business will grow.

The same thing can be said about the technology that we use to connect to the internet. iPhones, iPads, and other wireless devices can in fact become your mobile office. You can almost run your entire business from these devices. However, many people use them to just socialize, get into drama, and other things that are not conducive to their growth—not to mention spending hours upon hours playing games. You might think that you're having fun, but soon you will realize that while you were playing games you "got played" by spending your time unproductively. This is time that you cannot get back.

Today we are living in a global economy. To empower ourselves, we must know how to work the Net. Be careful how you build your online profiles.

110

Don't underestimate the value of these seemingly small things. There are millions of connections on social media: LinkedIn 75 million; Facebook 1 billion; and Twitter 150 million. The possibilities of potential connections are endless. Remember to always remain professional and to wear your professional hat. Having friends and meeting new friends or old classmates is nice, but what is your professional brand? What is your career or job? You don't have to be extremely serious, but you should always remember to walk that fine line of professionalism versus trying to be socially cool. Don't mix your online social life with your online professional presence. You should have a business Facebook profile and personal Facebook profile. Don't mix the two. Make sure all others like Twitter, LinkedIn, Google+, and Instagram are kept strictly professional. What you do or say can affect not only your professional profile, but also your business and your bottom line.

Stay Relevant

Phaedra Parks from the Real Housewives of Atlanta once said, "If people are not talking about you, you're just not relevant." You have to keep relevant. You must stay current with all of your marketing efforts, both online and off. Make sure to actively blog, tweet and post. Doing these things helps to keep your brand alive. What have you done lately? Remember: Being current will bring you currency, and that is your ultimate goal.

Gone Fishing

Networking is like fishing. You must be the bait. What is your lure? How do you reel them (clients, business, and leads) in? What's your pitch? Remember: You don't want to just jump on any fishing pole because not every lead is good for your business. Make sure that you're always sending out the right message because you want the right opportunities to come your way. Not all opportunities are the best ones for you and your business.

Steer Your Networking Ship

Make sure that you're the captain of your networking ship. Always steer it in the right direction. Remember that you're at the center of it all. Determine what offline events are the right ones for you to attend. Networking events are happening every day, but not all of them are good for your business or niche. Do your research and make sure that you attend those events that have the potential to increase your bottom line.

The fact of the matter is that businesses can't grow without the networking. This is a reality, and the sooner most small business owners accept it and start working it, the faster they will be able to see an increase in their bottom line. My best advice to readers is to monetize—or as I like to say, Mo-Net-tize—your networking activities both online and offline and see an instant increase. At the end of the day, you should know that widespread advertising, viral marketing, or competitive promotions in conjunction with unique branding can all be productive, but until you add networking, you will not see your business soar to new heights.

Networking comes in many forms: direct marketing, affiliate relationships, or even referrals. All of these are effective methods for getting new clients and developing new relationships. They all help grow your business or net worth. The truth is that working your Net (online) life can give you your best (business) life.

Assess and Adjust Your Network

You might have a small network of friends, affiliates, colleagues, clients, stakeholders, and partners or you might have a large one. Irrespective of the size, you should assess how your network is performing. Size really doesn't matter, and you should always endeavor to increase the outreach of your network and have more members with focused interests. If your present network is not generating results, then it's time to get a new network. Networking is not just about developing hundreds of connections; it's about forging relationships that are mutually rewarding. Networking is the new way to create your own Black Book. Many professional friendships are the result of expanding networks. Being laser focused can and will open many, and behind these doors you will find the most awesome people ready to help propel you to your purpose.

I am where I am today because of the way I networked. I was speaking at an event when I met the incomparable Toni Coleman-Brown. We exchanged business cards, and I followed through with keeping in contact with her. I attended several of her empowering seminars. While attending these seminars, I got a chance to network with not only Toni, but also countless others. Staying connected afforded me the opportunity to be a part of this powerful anthology. So as you can see, networking is about more than going to functions and exchanging business cards. It is about forming professional relationships that will be conducive to advancing your business. Discover the power of networking today. Learn from the mentors in this book who have guided thousands to a whole new level of net worth. It's more than going to functions and exchanging business cards. It is forming professional relationships that will be conducive in you advancing your business clientele. "Your future can be interactive. How you act now will activate your future." Audrey Reed

Work your net and don't get caught in it!

TONI COLEMAN-BROWN

Toni Coleman-Brown is an author, coach and motivational speaker. She is also the CEO and founder of the Network for Women in Business, an online community for women business owners who seek affordable cutting-edge training and the ability to connect and advance with other like-minded individuals. The motto for the network is "We EDUCATE to ELEVATE women in business." Toni can be reached at toni@networkforwomeninbusiness.com. Toni lives in Queens, New York, with her husband and two daughters.

Follow me at:

Facebook: http://www.facebook.com/tonicolemanbrown

Twitter: http://www.twitter.com/tonibrown

Websites: www.networkforwomeninbusiness.com

www.tonicolemanbrown.com

www.networkforwomeninbusiness.com

CHAPTER 18

NETWORKING: IT'S NOT ABOUT YOU! IT'S ABOUT WHO YOU SERVE

by Toni Coleman-Brown

Get rid of the I's when networking because it's not about you. Yes. I said it. It's not about you. Most people prepare for networking events by thinking about what they're going to say when people ask them that infamous question, "So, what do you do?" They spend hours and hours preparing for their "elevator pitch" because they think that it's about them and what they do. But I dare to say that, if you make this one-degree shift, everything will change for you when you go out to network, and you will get more leads, clients, and prospects than you can ever imagine.

What is this one thing you may ask? Well, it's simply this. Shift the focus from what you do to whom you serve.

At this point, you might be wondering what the heck am I talking about? Follow along while I make myself very clear. You see, constantly thinking about what you want, what your goals are, and what you want to accomplish at networking events unfortunately might not always yield the success that you're looking for because the one thing that turns off a potential client or customer more than anything is feeling like they're just a statistic on your path to achieving your goals and that you don't care about them. Potential clients hate to feel like you're just trying to achieve YOUR goals and that you're not paying attention to THEIR needs.

Truth be told, customers and clients don't really care about you and your needs. They only care about themselves. And while they're at the networking event pushing what they have to offer, you're also at the same networking event pushing what you have to offer. This way, no one will ever win. Something has to give. Someone has to shift the focus to make it a win–win for everyone.

116

We did that at the Network for Women in Business with our networking events. We were able to shift the focus. Our networking events are done based on the biblical principle and the universal law of "giving" and "receiving." Our events always have an educational component, but when we launch into our networking segment of our events, we make it a win–win for all involved.

We do this by first making our guest write down on a piece of paper three to five things that they have to give. On the other side of the paper, we ask them to write down three to five things that they're looking to receive. We challenge people to give first before they seek to gain. We do it this way because it makes our events more about the potential customer/client than it is about having a 30-second elevator pitch.

This method of networking makes breaking the ice a whole lot easier, and it also makes people feel more relaxed. It tends to expand the conversation beyond the traditional "what do you do?" question. We encourage people to think not only about their business when they're writing down what they're looking to receive, but also about their passions and hobbies. Sometimes people are looking for a good gym or cooking class in addition to their next best client or customer. This broadens the mix of potential leads to a wider variety of participants and makes for such better networking.

Once the stage is set for this type of networking, it becomes much easier for you as an attendee to become in a sense the honey to the bee, and your ability to attract your ideal clients goes up tremendously. The event transforms into the type of environment where anyone can position him-/herself more as a problem solver or the person who has the cure to heal their potential new client's pains versus being the person simply pushing what you have to offer.

This process is done with ease and grace, especially when you use your third ear.

Huh? I know. You're most likely thinking, "What are you talking about, Toni?" What third ear?

Well, your third ear is the ear that is in the middle of the word H-**EAR**-T. What this means is to listen with your heart instead of with your bottom line in mind. It means showing people that you care. It's the only way you'll be able to truly transform someone's pain into pleasure.

In all honesty, when it comes down to their business, people are sensitive. As a business owner yourself, you can probably understand why. Most people start their business to fulfill a burning desire in their heart. There is usually something tugging on them internally that pulls them in the direction of their dreams. For most business owners, it's about fulfilling their God-given purpose in life. When they talk about their businesses, they often times light up like a Christmas tree. This is why it's important to really hear a potential customer when they're talking during a networking event.

Let's face it. It takes a lot of courage to start a business and fulfill what many believe to be their God-given purpose in life. So to go to a networking event and feel as if people don't really care about you and what you do can be very disappointing. But when you network our way, and when you're in alignment with your purpose, everything comes with ease. Networking comes more naturally and, as a result, work becomes play. Long gone is the uncomfortable feeling of talking to strangers about what you do; now it's more about sharing your testimony and about fulfilling your purpose in life.

Networking this way also allows you to attract the "right" people. The first thing that you have to understand when networking is that you're not really looking for everyone. You're looking for the people who are looking for you. It's not always about the Law of Attraction which states that likes will attract likes, which means that you will begin to attract people who are just like you. It's about knowing who is your ideal customer and being of service to them.

So, I'll say it again: In networking, it's not about you; it's about who you serve. Therefore, the next time you attend a networking event, instead of thinking about what you're going to say, think about: Who is your ideal customer? What is it that they want? What is it that they need? What is their biggest problem? Exactly how will you and your business or service solve their problem?

There is a famous statement that says, "Service is the rent you pay for living." I believe this quote. It is because of this quote that I launched the Network for Women in Business—so that I could be of service. I know exactly who it is that I serve and I know what my mission in life is. I am being true to myself and to my purpose, and it feels good. Networking is the center of it all for my business. It is not only how I add to my bottom line; it is an integral part of my bottom line and, without it, my business would not exist.

I can tell you countless stories of people whom I have connected and people who have connected people to me as a result of the Network for Women in Business. If it wasn't for this network I wouldn't have met Christine Marmoy, who is responsible for assisting me with this collaboration. If it wasn't for this network and the way we network, most of the women who are a part of this book wouldn't be here today.

So this book project is living proof of the power of networking not being about you, but being about who you serve. I am thankful to God for giving me the vision, the purpose, and the drive to pursue my passion of being of service to others and allowing me to serve in this way. And I am thankful to each of you for allowing me to serve you in this way.

JULIA D. SHAW

Julia D. Shaw has extensive experience serving as a PR and marketing consultant for more than 20 years in the publishing industry. She expanded her professional reach to include special events and non-profit management in addition to business consultation and coaching services for small businesses, non-profit organizations, and emerging professionals. Follow her blog at www.juleznewz.com for updates on her reinvention agenda. Contact her at juleznewz@gmail.com or 917-501-6780 for consultation services, speaking engagements, and book signings.

CHAPTER 19

REINVENTION: MY NETWORK CHANGED MY LIFE AND SO CAN YOURS!

by Julia D. Shaw

BABY BOOMERS RULE!!! Literally, one out of four Americans is a baby boomer, meaning he or she was born between 1946 and 1964. With such large statistics, this age group has influenced all aspects of popular culture and lifestyle. We (Yes! I am a baby boomer) believe that age is nothing but a number and doesn't define or limit who we are or what we will accomplish throughout our lifetime. We have embraced the idea of reinvention with the experience of an array of personal accomplishments and failures. Baby boomers are aggressively working to change the old-fashion mindset on aging in America today.

I am truly blessed to be a 53-year-old woman who happens to be African American and a proud single mother of two awesome adult daughters. Between them, I have three precious grandchildren. They are the foundation of my life. The support of my network, also known as the village, has helped me raise my children. I am an empty-nester, or as I like to say, I am "on the other side of motherhood" as the parent of grown children. The role I play in my two daughters' lives has changed, and all aspects of my life have changed as well. Being a mother has given me a defining inner voice in this world. My voice is that of encouragement to others to pursue their dreams in a realistic manner to increase their net worth by believing in themselves and others. This inner voice can also be heard in my management style.

My mother has several life lesson quotes that she lives by and shared with her children. The quote that was most impactful throughout my life is: "People will help you when you are trying to help yourself." Translated: Your network will help you when you are trying to help yourself. Reinventing myself includes the added support and insights of my professional network of mentors, managers, colleagues, co-workers, clients, contacts, and referrals also mixed in with my personal network of family, extended family, blended family, and ex-families connected to an array of cross-cultural friends and friends of friends. My network multiplies with an introduction to one or two people in their networks, which can be helpful to me or I can be helpful to them.

The concept of reinvention is the positive opportunity to embrace change. The bottom line is that reinvention is a fancy word for doing things differently by incorporating previous life experiences in the decision-making process. Reinvention is being proactive to change rather than being reactive. Reinvention is choosing change rather than having it forced upon us. Reinvention is exploring your options, then making the choice that you think is best for your current aspirations and lifestyle. Reinvention is thinking through the process of change and being engaged with planning the desired outcomes because we all know that "you can't do the same thing expecting different results" or set goals and do nothing toward making them a reality. It is important not to look at reinvention negatively.

Thirty years ago, my career path rotated around having flexibility in my schedule to be hands-on when raising my daughters. Entrepreneurship provided me that opportunity. I was an entrepreneurial workaholic working toward my goal of building a business as a literary publicist and event manager. The African American publishing marketplace was a promising and growing niche within the publishing industry; authors were going on multiple city book tours, conducting book signings and media interviews nationally and internationally. I worked for a number of radio stations, expos, special events, conferences, publishers, and authors. Business was growing.

Then circumstances beyond anyone's control created a shift in the publishing industry. The first shift was the impact of the bombing of the World Trade Center on September 11, 2001, causing marketing budgets and book tours to be reduced. The second shift was the introduction of new technology such as print-on-demand publishing, e-books, the internet, and numerous emerging social media platforms. These fast-paced changes impacted the literary publicity market as well as book marketing and promotion throughout book publishing and sales.

The impact of these shifts had a negative impact on my cash flow over several years and made me realize that, as much as I loved what I was doing, I needed to explore ways to reinvent my entrepreneurial passion. So during the process of reinvention, I decided that after 20 years it was time to get a full-time, 9-to-5 day job.

I began the quest the only way I knew how: through my network. I let everyone I came into contact with know that I was planning to make a change and get a job until I figured things out. My first interview was a referral through my network, and I got the job.

Now, I had time to reflect back on my life and, in 2009, decided to return to college and complete my Bachelors of Science degree in Business Administration—after a 23-year "leave of absence." At first I was nervous about returning to college at age 50, but I also felt that it was important to complete my college degree. Within my network I have a former client and friend who is the Chair of the Teacher Education Department at York College. She encouraged me and helped me with the process of seeing what credits I needed to graduate. Her support through the three years was priceless.

Completing my degree took a lot of time and energy. Along the way, I got discouraged sometimes and beat up on myself for not doing this sooner or when I was younger like everyone else. I had to make sacrifices, not participating in many family activities, parties, conferences, and events. I even had to end a relationship with a man who needed more attention than I could give because school work came first. At times I wanted to quit, but a chance meeting with someone in my network who told me how proud they were of me for going back to school got me back on track.

I value the knowledge and experience gained when I returned to college; couple that with my life experience and you get an investment in my net worth that reinforces the fact that I can do anything, regardless of how long it takes. I started York College in Jamaica, New York, in 1978 after graduating from high school. I graduated from York College in 2012. Walking across the stage in my cap and gown among all those beautiful young folks that I had shared classes with and shaking the hand of the college president was a simple gesture, but a defining moment of the completion and reinvention for me.

I have learned to embrace change and find the lesson and the blessing in the most unexpected people and places. We try to ink our life into existence, but in reality we should learn to script life in pencil with a big eraser. Accept that the book of life is written in pencil and, when needed, we can change or rearrange a sentence, edit a page, or rewrite a chapter—all of which is the blessing of reinvention.

What's next on my reinvention agenda, you ask? I have always wanted to be an author! Being part of the network of powerful women in this book and sharing a small part of my life experiences are part of my reinvention. Now I get the opportunity to promote my book! I have always told people that when I retired I wanted to be an artist and do oil paintings on the beach. Well, this baby boomer isn't retiring any time soon, but I want to be an artist! I want to have an art exhibit in a gallery and even sell a piece of my artwork. Over the years I have connected with a number of artists and plan to tap into that network shortly. What is on your reinvention agenda? If I can do it, so can you!

LUCRECE AUGUSMA

A native of Port-au-Prince, Haiti, Lucrece Augusma is an entrepreneur, educator, and performing artist. She is the CEO of Envisi8 Solutions, a business and media consulting firm helping entrepreneurs build their organizations and providing tools to help them bring their vision to pass. She is also the vice-chairperson on the WHOP Academy Board. In her spare time, she sings with an award-winning local gospel group in Miami, Florida, and teaches liturgical dance at her church.

E-mail: alucrece.whopa@gmail.com

Facebook: https://www.facebook.com/lucrece.augusma

Twitter: https://twitter.com/GreatnessMay7

LinkedIn: http://www.linkedin.com/in/envisi8

CHAPTER 20

NETWORKING 20/20: CONNECT YOUR NETWORK TO YOUR VISION

by Lucrece Augusma

Imagine purchasing a brand new television on sale for only $100. You reach for the plug and head to the outlet to begin enjoying your TV and, behold, the plug does not match the power outlet! It can be like that sometimes in your networking endeavors, especially if your network is not connected to your vision.

What is Vision?

Vision is the starting point in achieving great things. Vision is the art of seeing the invisible, beginning with the end in mind. Vision unites people together for one common objective, casting all self-serving desires and personal agendas aside. Vision fulfillment can be activated by your aspirations followed by a strong, dedicated, and unselfish supporting cast: your network.

How does vision relate to networking? As previously stated, without the right people supporting your vision, it will be difficult for your vision to pass. Therefore, you must build a network that wants to associate with you because they see a potential to accomplish something great together. Bringing a vision to reality is not a one-person show, but a rallying of individuals who see what you see for your company.

The Vision and Network Connection

When I was searching for a true definition of networking, many of the statements seemed very impersonal and self-centered. But I came across one that made an indelible impression, changing my whole outlook on networking. According to Ivan Misner, networking is "the process of developing and activating your relationships to increase your business, enhance your knowledge, expand your sphere of influence or serve the community." Networking is all about relationships, and those relationships should be built upon a shared vision. Connecting the right people with what you see for your company is an important step toward fulfilling your vision as a business and an expert in your field.

Vision Partners vs. Vision Quenchers

In my networking quests, I like to separate potential relationships into two categories: Vision Partners and Vision Quenchers. A network that sees your vision can help bring your company forward. They have your best interest at heart and have a genuine motivation to help you succeed. They are not only in it for association, but by purpose. These are the Vision Partners. One Vision Partner can connect you to others who probably share the same vision. This will, in turn, bring your business to greater heights. In contrast, a Vision Quencher only wants to connect with you for their own self-interests, and not for a greater purpose. Don't get me wrong, making money is important, but that shouldn't be where the line is drawn in the sand.

Ask yourself these questions:

- Do they share my values and philosophy?
- They have a lot of capital I can probably benefit from, but is their integrity in tact?
- How is our relationship going to help other people succeed?

It is my personal philosophy that businesses should be in business to make lives better. Our businesses should be a platform for bringing solutions to society's challenges. Although we can't cure every ill, as business owners we can still make a positive difference. Therefore, if you want to connect with me, you have to align with this vision.

Dangers of a Vision Quencher

To illustrate the point of connecting with the right people, I want to share something that happened to my mother. My mother has been an entrepreneur since I was born—literally. She worked hard building a company that provided a variety of wholesale specialty foods and drinks. In addition, she also had a thriving catering company that served the Haitian-American community in South Florida. She amassed a following and generated a lucrative income from these businesses. Her hard work and dedication brought her to the point where she was able to have her own storefront establishment.

One day at a local social event, she met this woman (for the sake of anonymity, we'll call her Jan) who was also an entrepreneur. They struck up a conversation about their business endeavors. Both women found mutual ground where they both wanted to make more money. After many conversations, they decided to become business partners. At this point, however, my mother failed to explain the vision of her company to Jan. She did not communicate that she built her business on integrity and principles. Her eagerness at what Jan promised financially seemed to overshadow what really mattered: the company's vision.

Soon they rented a place near our home, purchased materials to remodel, and began promoting the grand opening. Eventually the business launched and, over time, my mother began to notice some disturbing things. It came to light that Jan's dealings were far from ethical, and it was apparent that Jan was completing transactions that benefitted her best interests and not the company. From unfulfilled promises to connecting with unreliable suppliers, it was evident that this network surrounding my mother included wolves in sheep's clothing. This brought a significant strain on the partnership and the business. After one year, my mother backed out of the partnership, which cost her thousands of dollars. Those dollars could have been saved if Jan and her connections had aligned with my mother's vision of business integrity.

Fortunately, my mother was able to recuperate from this downfall. She got back up and began to build more positive relationships. Upon initial contact with potential investors, she made her vision and direction clear right off the bat. As a result, she was able to secure distribution contracts with several local specialty foods distributors. Her business became profitable again, and the rest is history. That's the power of the vision and network connection!

5 Tips for Vision-Driven Networking

Based on prior experience, I summarized the process of connecting your network with your vision in five simple tips:

1. Outline a clear vision of your company, providing the direction you want your company to go. Make that vision clear when networking with potential Vision Partners.

2. Make a list of the ideal types of people who you see can fit in your network. These are people you know that, if you have them on board, their partnership can propel you toward attaining your vision.

3. Separate the wheat from the chaff. When you come from a networking event, sit down, evaluate, and sift through every connection you've made. Make two piles: the Potential Vision Partner pile and the Vision Quencher pile.

4. When networking, pay attention to what is being said. Studies show that most people make decisions about a person within the first 30 seconds to 2 minutes of interaction. Use that to your advantage; take notes and focus on details.

5. Did a connection not work out for you? Don't worry. Not everyone is meant to be in your circle. As you will learn in the next section, some people are not meant to stay with you on your road to success.

Prayer: The Real Connection

As I close this chapter, I decided to leave the best for last. Many can attest to the fact that prayer is powerful. This might not be a popular strategy for some or written in the big guru books, but it works for me. Prayer is the first thing that should be done before venturing out on any project. The Good Book says, "In all our ways acknowledge Him, and He shall direct thy paths." If you are networking with vision, guidance and counsel are essential in making the right decisions.

It's important to realize that God is writing a beautiful story with you as the lead character. Your supporting cast must be strategically placed to bring you toward your destiny. The only one who knows what is best for you is God Himself. Something as simple as praying before an event can help you weed out the good from the bad. Prayer builds your discernment and keeps you focused on what to look for. To tell the truth, I don't want to make the same mistakes my mother and countless others made by jumping in head first without consulting with my Father. Is it possible to have a bad apple in the bunch? Of course it's possible. We're human and sometimes, because of sheer excitement, we tend to ignore subtle discrepancies. But even wrong connections can be turned around for the betterment of your business as long as you place God in control.

The reason why I am so passionate about this subject is because prayer is what brought me here to this point. Prayer is what connected me to the right people, which in turn, steered me in the right direction. Who would've thought that, in 2013, I would be co-authoring a book with other remarkable women dreamers, visionaries, movers, and shakers? The real power in connecting your network with your vision is not in your charisma. It is not how you can master a conversation and persuade people or how much money your connection has. It's connecting with the vision that God has for you.

I am a living witness that, when you ask God to order your steps, He will set you before the kings and nobles of this world, no matter who you are—rich, poor, black, white, red, orange, or blue! As vision is the art of seeing the invisible, it takes a different set of eyes to envision. Without the Invisible, we can't see the invisible. That's why, when you have God in the equation, your network connections can't go wrong.

POLLY HADFIELD

An administrator with an entrepreneurial spirit and more than 30 years of experience, Polly Hadfield has led and trained successful teams in both the administrative arena and network marketing. Polly and her husband run a successful home-based public adjusting business that educates property owners about their insurance policies and, in the event of a covered loss, assists them in obtaining their full entitlement. They have built their business on integrity, hard work, and respect.

Email: Pollymetropa@gmail.com

Website: www.metropa.com/kenandpolly

Facebook: https://www.facebook.com/polly.hadfield

Linkedin: http://www.linkedin.com/in/PollyHadfield

CHAPTER 21

REFERRALS!
REFERRALS!
REFERRALS!

by Polly Hadfield

The Mastermind principle consists of an
alliance of two or more minds working in perfect
harmony for the attainment of a common definite
objective. Success does not come without the
cooperation of others.
–Napoleon Hill

NEVER NEVER NEVER NEVER NEVER
NEVER NEVER give up!
–Sir Winston Churchill

Ask, Ask, Ask

When my husband and I attended a holiday party for our new home-based business 11 years ago, our intentions were to boldly meet and talk to all the "big names" in the business that we had read about on the company website. One of the biggest names in the company at that time was standing by the bar, and we went right over to him, shook his hand, and introduced ourselves. Not wanting to monopolize his time, and not wanting to look like green "newbies," we asked just one question and were hoping for the answer that would unlock all the secrets and put us instantly on a successful path: How are you so successful? He looked at us and said there are three words you need to know. We leaned in for his answer. We knew it would be "the" answer, we could just feel it! He said in a casual but authoritative voice with years of experience behind it: referrals, referrals, referrals. We looked at each other and then at him and nodded as if we fully understood the ins and outs and depth of his answer. We really didn't have a clue but "never let them see you sweat," right? Little did we know that once we understood those three words and the power they held, we would be on our way and would never look back!

It's who you know, right? We've all heard this before. But did you know that's not necessarily the truth? How about who *they* know? Some of you will remember the shampoo commercial: They tell two friends, who tell two friends, and so on and so on. (I know, I'm dating myself.)

There is nothing stronger than a referral or recommendation. Whether it is for a job, introduction, product, or service, a referral represents a higher probability of success by virtue of familiarity and trust.

There is a secret I will share with you on how to get referrals later in this chapter.

There are two sources for referrals. The one we'll address first is your current clients. By far the most powerful thing you can have when approaching new people is a referral from their colleagues, friends, or others they respect. Most people assume that referrals will happen by themselves if you provide good customer service. This isn't true. If you are not deliberate and proactive in creating referrals, the chances of receiving as many referrals as you want are slim. You must create a referral process that works for you and your business. A client that refers you will be a loyal business client and is more apt to use you again in the future, so you want to be sure you have your clients referring you to their family and friends. When someone is referred by someone they trust, they are less likely to shop around further or look for a better price. This type of referral carries a high level of credibility.

It's very important to stay in contact with your clients. Thank you cards after they use your service, holiday cards, an occasional email with updates on your service, and other simple but effective communications are all great ways to stay in touch without being a nuisance. Your professionalism will speak volumes with these actions. And always remember to say thank you for any referrals you receive.

Very often, the same question comes up: How do I get more referrals? My answer is always the same: Ask for them. Remember the secret I said I would share with you on how to get referrals? That was it—just ask for them. It really is that simple. Our nature is to want to help people who have helped us. Asking for referrals occasionally will only get you occasional referrals. You can get many more valuable referrals by asking regularly. Asking for referrals is hands-down the most commonly neglected step. Too many salespeople are so relieved to get a sale that they grab their things and race out the door the second they get the chance out of fear that the prospect will change their mind! This is where your passion and enthusiasm for your product come in. Your client will see the belief and excitement you have for your product and you won't need to "run for the door"!

The way you ask for referrals also affects the results. Asking "Do you know anyone who could use my service?" won't give you the desired results because it's too broad. It is a closed question to which it is easy to say "no." People need a specific frame of reference to help them think of possible referral candidates. One example would be, "Is there a neighbor of yours that might have experienced the same issue and could benefit from my service?" This allows the person to "see" the potential referrals in their mind.

The best thing about referrals is that they are free. Don't make the mistake of giving referral fees. This typically ends badly. It breaks the trust that is automatic with referrals and therefore destroys the relationship you have worked to build. A fee also belittles the value of your product or service.

My sister has owned a business forms distributorship for the last 30 years. The first year her business was 5% referral and 95% cold calling; now it is just the opposite. She also owns a bed and breakfast in Newport, Rhode Island, and—because of website reviews from past guests—her business is almost totally based on referrals. How did she manage to garner so many reviews on her website? Simple: She asked her guests.

Partners in Profit

Your best referral sources are, of course, your customers. They are the people who have experienced the quality of your product and service. The second source for referrals is influential people. Look beyond your customer base to find referral partners. Be creative! There are many other people and organizations that you should include in your referral process. These are people who know and mingle with many other influential people. They are the heavy hitters who can have a profound multiplying effect on your business. A smart business owner will spend the majority of their referral prospecting time with 20% of these people as these 20% will produce 80% of the results.

Some of these people will be directly related to your business in some way (perhaps offering complimentary products and services). Others are people you come into contact with on a regular basis in your everyday life, but aren't connected to your industry. These people also connect with a large number of other people and they too can multiply your marketing efforts.

So it stands to reason that building strong referral partners should be on your "to do" list. They need to understand your business so their referrals will carry weight and make sense. I find that people want to refer you, but aren't sure exactly how to refer you or perhaps don't fully understand what you do. If you want more referrals, you will need to educate your referral partners. Help them to help you.

Collaboration is key to building strong relationships. Collaboration, at its core, is people interacting with people. I referenced a quote by Napoleon Hill at the start of this chapter: Essentially, two heads are better than one (you learned that in kindergarten when you learned not to run with scissors and how to color inside the lines). Smarter collaboration enables people to access the right people or information when they need it. Create a collaborative climate. Offer your assistance to others. Prove that you are trustworthy. Respect others. Be consistent in your behavior and the way you respond to others.

Reconnect with people. You will be amazed at what doors will open. A reconnection is exactly how I came to collaborate on this book.

Final Thoughts

After a few years of experience, I realized that it's not the numbers that count, but the quality of relationships I nurtured. To be a great networker you must become focused on others and not on yourself. Zig Ziglar once said, "You can get everything in life you want if you just help enough other people get what they want."

It all comes down to the passion you have. Get behind something you are passionate about and share it with everyone. You will be amazed at the results. Meeting that top income earner 11 years ago has shaped our business success in ways we couldn't have imagined!

> *There are three classes of people: Those who see. Those*
> *who see when they are shown. Those who do not see.*
> –Leonardo da Vinci

CHIKEOLA KARIMOU

Chikeola Karimou loves supporting new paradigm entrepreneurs and visionaries create A Stellar Life—one where they stand radiantly in their power and function powerfully like a CEO. An expert in vision clarity and self-confidence building, she shows people how to open up to their abundance. Her dream life started when she stepped forward and claimed her vision. She now shows others how to do the same.

Website: www.thestellarceo.com

Facebook: www.facebook.com/thestellarceo

Twitter: @Be1StellarCEO

Email: IbecomingStellar@gmail.com

CHAPTER 22

GIFTING YOU: SERVICE & GENEROSITY AS NETWORKING

by Chikeola Karimou

I like to think of some aspects of my life as mini love stories. Please allow me the opportunity to broaden and expand your vision of love stories and understand that I am moving them out of the box of the romantic kind. I mean, what are the stories we tend to get attached to in our lives? They usually tend to revolve around romance, do they not? I cherish the idea of creating a life that is fun, full of adventures, deeply meaningful, and fulfilling. So I look at the events and happenings in my life and wonder about the ones I can keep going back to because they inspire me, uplift me, and remind me when I forget about how to always stay connected to my values.

Here is one story I'll never forget. I had just transitioned from living on the East Coast to starting over on the West Coast. After 18 years on the East Coast, first in New York City then Greenwich, Connecticut, I left for the West Coast, answering something inside of me that knew it was time for change and following a desire I had been keeping quiet for far too long. I found Bellingham, Washington, and moved. Once here, the advice I consistently received from all the well-wishers welcoming me into the community was to network—to get out and get to know people. Being the good student that I am, I followed the advice that was given to me and dutifully and diligently put myself out there. It was at one such gathering/networking event that I met this lovely woman, whom I will call Ether Rose, who is now a very good friend of mine.

At the networking event that night, there were many of us. It was business oriented, and we were all busy passing our business cards around and speaking to impress—or at least that was my understanding of what I was supposed to do. Of course we also sought out how to find ways to have good leads become clients. Ether Rose was this tall, full-bodied woman with lots of light and radiance and, through our conversation, I discovered that we had New York City in common. She had moved to Bellingham a couple of years prior and naturally, having New York City as a link, we decided to stay in touch, get together for coffee, and reminisce about our dear Big Apple that we both somehow still missed. Somewhere in that conversation, she mentioned that she was in the process of moving and that it might take a week or two before we could connect. Spontaneously, I offered: Don't hesitate to ask if you need help; I am happy to help. Moving requires a lot of energy, and I am always happy to help a friend. And that was the beginning of our friendship

Through my connection with Ether Rose, I attended a learning event, and that's where it happened. The presenter was brilliant at what she was sharing and teaching us, but for some reason, I kept feeling her being uncomfortable at a level I am not sure she even realized herself. For me, that underlying feeling—totally unconscious to her—was completely ruining my experience of her because, instead of listening to what she was saying, I kept wondering about what her problem could be. Eventually I realized that I could either stay in that energy of wondering what was wrong with the picture of this person looking so successful on the outside yet not really in her power deeply within or I could do something about it. I decided to do something about it. At the end of the lecture, I went to her and plainly told her I wanted to work with her. This person became my first high-end client at over $5 K. Beyond the money, this gave me the opportunity to serve someone at a level I had only dreamt about before. I was offering my skills and talents in a way that was making my heart sing. I was receiving validation in the outer world that something I was holding in my heart was possible—and not only was it possible, there were actually people out there who would enjoy it. I realized at that moment, that there are people out there who needed what I had to offer. How sweet! And it all started because I offered my help to a total stranger.

So here is what I desire to share with all of you:

1. **Emulate Nature: Understand and Align Yourself with the Flow of Life.** In other words, Gift yourself whenever you can. Look around and you will notice that we are gifted everything—be it the sun, the trees, the wind, the water, the breath we breathe...everything.

I know it might not seem that way, especially when things are not where we would like them to be, and maybe that is part of the lesson here. It might look like on the surface that we are making things happen, but we are being called here to look a bit deeper and we will see that all is happening through us and that we are provided for. One of the secrets of being provided for abundantly is for us to also be willing to provide to others.

2. **Keeping the Heart Open.** In other words, trust that spontaneous energy thrust from your heart and go with it. This aspect of the process is so important. It's a Thrust and Trust thing. This requires that we be present in our bodies and acknowledge as well as recognize the quick movement that comes and asks us to take action. I know I have seen this in myself so many times and, if you are like me, I am sure it has happened to you as well. We receive an insight. It is quick and subtle and, before we know it, we start debating if we should follow it or not. The answer is yes. Learn to follow your inner guidance, and that means learn to leave your mind out of this and know your values.

3. **Honoring the Oneness of All of Life.** What I noticed with us conscious entrepreneurs is that we are aware that there is no Life at home, Life at the office, Life at church, and so on. We are understanding that there is LIFE and this Life is expressed through us through everything we do. Clearly, the old paradigm of adopting a certain way of being and behaving in one's private life and acting in another way in one's business life is shifting. We cannot be wonderful human beings on Sundays but throat-cutting sharp business owners on Monday. It seems that value system is not working for us as a whole anymore, which is why so many of us are now inviting people to live a conscious life. Honor the Oneness of Life and embody your values in all aspects of your life; avoid creating categories and disconnection. On the contrary, see yourself as the One Life giving you opportunities to express all your values and all that matters to you through every single aspect of your life.

4. **The Law of Circulation: Know and Understand it**. Yes, give and give and give; Yes, it will come back to you. No, it might not come back to you through the person you gave to. Like so many people

I have observed around me, do not fall into the mistaken idea that when you give, it has to come back to you through that person. It might or it might not. From my experience though, and through the teachers and books I have received from in the last 25 years, it does not work that way. We give, let go joyfully, and it will find a way to come back to us joyfully, especially when we are doing so genuinely from our heart. What I mean here is do not have an agenda. Of course, I am not saying that we cannot have an agenda sometimes, as this is part of business savvy through joint ventures and various partnerships. Even at that level, what I am saying is that, if one is controlling and calculating, it does not unfold the same way as when one is simply being in one's heart, moving, gifting, participating from a place of Being You.

5. **Gifting as you would love to receive.** We all know this one: "Do unto others as you would love done unto you." This one is really quite simple. Even if you know you are out there gifting you as a practice, do it full heartedly. Do whatever it is you are doing the way you would love it to be done to you and have fun while at it. This flows into the next point…

6. **Giving from a place of Service, Generosity, and Love.** As I was writing, I wondered if this particular point was necessary, if I was being redundant. I am realizing maybe not, and here is why. Above, I am asking you to give as you would like to receive, and that is true. Here, I am calling your attention to remembering to also hold the inner space of I am in Service here and I desire to be generous. By holding this space, you are remembering to help the person the way they desire to be helped. This has happened, so it is not superficial. You might be having an idea about how things should go or be done, etc., and the person you are helping might be asking you to go about it in a particular way. It might not be to your liking. Sometimes, you might even be out helping and the people you are helping might not even be courteous. This is the place where, if you remember you are being of service and giving generously, you will not let an incident or anything get in the way of you having fun while gifting of you.

7. **Nurturing your connections.** Life gets busy. We get busy. This one seems like one of those impossible tasks set before us. How

can we nurture all our connections? Is that even possible? What I have noticed in my experience is that Life has a way of ebbing and flowing people in and out of our life. So to start, you might want to notice which people are being brought into your life, what they are about, and what it is that they are contributing to you at this particular period of your life. Find a way to stay open to the "gifts" they have for you. Pay attention here, Dear One, and notice I put into quotes the word gift. There is a part of my psyche that wants to associate gift with pleasant and sweet. This is not always so. Truly, it is all good. Attached to nurturing your connections is the practice of not taking anything personally. Some of the people who come into our lives bring some gifts that are not beautifully wrapped at first. If you are able to stay with it and see beyond the packaging, you will get to the nectar.

A business-savvy move for us conscious entrepreneurs is to constantly remember and choose to practice the knowing of the Interconnectedness of All of Life. With that knowledge, and remembering our first foundation to "Emulate Nature", we practice staying open and receiving all the gifts, no matter how wrapped they came, digging for the good we know resides within without closing any doors. Remember, Emulate Nature. See as Life sees, give as Life gives.

MARSHA GRAHAM

Marsha, the founder of Virtual MediClaims, is an experienced medical coder specializing in medical billing and patient statements. Virtual MediClaims provides ecommerce solutions for small to mid-size businesses that streamline their business operations, resulting in an improvement to their bottom line. She assists clients to accept payments everywhere in many platforms online and mobile. She earned her Medical Coding Certificate from Richland College, and she graduated with a Bachelor of Science degree in Technical Management from DeVry University. Marsha lives in Dallas, Texas. You can reach her by:

Email: virtualmediclaims@gmail.com

Facebook: www.facebook.com/virtualmediclaims

Twitter: @Mediclaims

CHAPTER 23

NETWORKING: SOMETIMES IT'S BETTER ONLINE

by Marsha Graham

In 1991, I decided I wanted my own business because it was the second time in 10 years that I had been laid off from my job in the banking industry. I realized it was time to look again to find employment in a more stable industry. At that time, opportunities were being reported in the health care industry, and there were training schools advertising that there was good money to be made working at home doing medical billing.

So my friends and I started looking for medical billing training. There were so many from which to choose. I responded to a home-study program listed in a local newspaper. According to the ad, their manual would include training on how to start a medical billing company, a list of doctors in the area, and the software to process insurance claims. This sounded reasonable, so I mailed them my money and waited. It didn't go well. After several phone calls, they finally mailed me the manual on a CD, but with no software and the information was so worthless that I could have obtained it for free somewhere else.

I learned from that little episode and decided to enroll in a local program. I attended Concorde Career Institute and earned my certificate in medical office management in October 1992. After receiving this training, I still didn't know much about running a small business. Then I attended a variety of business training seminars in the local community. I discovered that there are many things that a business owner has to do in order to have a successful and profitable business. As a solo entrepreneur, whether providing a service or a product, it takes a solid business plan, capital, equipment and supplies, and a marketing plan to sustain a successful business.

To further develop my expertise, in August 1998, I earned my certificate from Richland College as a medical records coding specialist. I really enjoyed going to college and would look for the best instructors. For instance, during my last year in the program, one of my final required courses was anatomy and physiology. I heard there was an instructor at another community college who was much better than the instructor teaching this course at Richland. The course was offered in the summer, so I found a part-time medical billing job to gain practical experience and quit my full-time job to attend summer school. I loved that course and learning about the wonders of the body Our Creator has given all of us. Truly amazing...

Within months of completing the program at Richland, I had a full-time position in an orthopedic office because they were looking for a billing specialist who had medical billing training and experience. This is where I gained additional experience in outpatient and surgery experience for which I account my success in coding, posting payments and account receivables. After working in the health care industry for three years, I continued to broaden my knowledge base and attended the Practice Management Institute, earning my certificate as a medical coder in May 2001.

In 2001, I started building my own full-time business while working temporary jobs. In the meantime, I was working with a couple of network marketing companies to generate cash flow for my business. Unfortunately, I found I was spending more time and money on these part-time ventures than on developing my business. I realized I needed to let go of this work if my own business was to truly grow.

Gradually, I let these side jobs go, but my friends kept calling me with the next best thing and asking me if I was making the kind of money I wanted to be making. And I would respond, "Not yet." It would have been more helpful if my friends had said, "Marsha, you will get there, just keep doing what you do best." Don't fall for that "next best thing" distraction because it will side track you for weeks or maybe months. You won't have reached your goals and the year will be half over. When you are taking your business to the next level, stay focused on your passion and your business plan goals to reach momentum in your business.

Before I started my business to process medical insurance claims for health care providers, I researched the best medical billing software. I chose

MediSoft® because it was very popular, was taught at colleges, and was user-friendly and easy to learn. Also, at that time it was free to be a reseller, and there were no sales quota required. As a MediSoft® reseller in Dallas, Texas, I was listed in their online directory. That was my first experience with networking online. Being listed in that online directory changed everything for me. Whenever I got a lead to sell the software, I would not only install it, but also train the doctor's staff to use the software to process clean medical claims following the insurance carriers' guidelines for rapid reimbursement. Of all the many different ways that I tried to secure some medical billing contracts, most of my contracts were a byproduct of selling MediSoft® software to health care providers and being listed in their online directory.

Offline networking also played a very important part in building my client base. When I am networking for potential clients, I attend as many networking events as possible around my work schedule. I go with the expectation of meeting potential clients such as chiropractors and therapists, and other small business owners who offer business services to assist me in running my own business more efficiently. Many times when I go with the intention to find a particular product or services, there is usually a company in attendance with whom I can connect. Sometimes I go just to see who is still in business. Either way, I always meet someone who can help me— whether it's a small business owner who offers business cards, computer services, or marketing. Just recently I attended an event and met some sales representatives for a marketing company that has put my business online using videos and social media.

My ideal customers, doctors and chiropractors, were not at the networking events that I was attending. So I started searching for where they might convene or get together. As I was networking with other medical billers, they mentioned that the chiropractic college has vendor expos for the students before they graduate. I immediately scheduled my first vendor table at the chiropractic college expo. A few chiropractors showed interest and requested information about the medical billing software more than my billing services. It led to several software sales. A year later after attending that event, someone who kept my business card called, and that was the making of my second big contract. This taught me to always focus on my passion, network with my target customers, always have plenty of business cards, and follow-up with potential clients.

TANESHA WILLIAMS

Tanesha Williams has been employed at Downstate Hospital for more than 10 years. She is a certified health coach and a licensed Zumba instructor. She is a member of Health Fairs Direct, Inc., setting up wellness workshops for companies as a wellness coordinator to help boost employee attendance and morale. She is a state-licensed financial representative, helping clients plan and save for retirement.

Ms. Williams is also the personal assistant and armor bearer to Bishop Seabrooks and has been a member of the Rehoboth Cathedral for more than 10 years. She has overcome life's challenges and has leaped over hurdles to improve her life. Her story is one of strength and victory. She is motivated to take her business to another level and to encourage single parents that, no matter what you face, God will make a way. She loves to sing, dance, and ride her bike in her spare time. She is the proud parent of two beautiful daughters. Her motto is if you can believe it, you can achieve it. She is currently working on launching her business The Wellness Club to encourage, motivate, and support women.

CHAPTER 24

SUCCESSFUL NETWORKING WITH A PURPOSE

by Tanesha Williams

But seek ye first the kingdom of
God and his righteousness, and all these
things shall be added unto you.
–Matthew 6:33

Networking is a tool that should be used daily—in the grocery store, at the car wash, and yes, even at the gym. Always be on the lookout for people who have a pleasant smile on their face in order to engage them in a conversation. That is an opportunity to introduce yourself and your business, so make sure to take it at every chance you can get

I have discovered that it is impossible to grow a business or even a career without networking. When I began working at Downstate Hospital, my mind was set on getting to work every day on time and being prepared to stay late if needed. I quickly learned that networking and talking to people were essential parts of my job. Working at Downstate requires me to speak with patients, family members, and other staff relating to the care of the patient. My goal has always been to be unselfish in finding the best resources for our patients. I have been able to use that same energy and skill set to build a solid business.

I've been blessed to be able to pursue my passion while being employed full-time. You must be in a good position in your life in order to take on new adventures. You shouldn't do so if you're not going to personally invest time into it. I was able to grow my business and sustain my job at Downstate because I could rely on family and friends—in other words, my personal network—for encouragement.

At Downstate Hospital, there are people dealing with many infirmities. Some patients have lost their mobility; many are feeble and weak. At one time I felt like I had lost my own personal vision. I had to ask myself, "Why am I not growing"? I felt like a part of me was shrinking because there was no growth taking place in my life. It felt as if my business was not prospering and my vision was cloudy. So I had to take the necessary steps to get my vision back on track. These are some steps that I will offer to you just in case you also feel as if you've lost your way and you want to get back on track.

Rely on Your Network and Believe in Yourself

I remember when I sat down with my very first client. I knew my goal was to put a life insurance policy in place for the family. I knew what I had to do, but fear almost stopped me. Listening to my mind could have talked me out of helping a family and myself out of a sale. But I didn't let it happen. I believed in myself. If you ever find yourself in this position, don't allow yourself to be moved by what you see, but by what you believe. Good things come to those who work through their fears.

Have Faith and Confidence

Have enough confidence in God to know that, whatever you desire, God will bring it to pass in your life. You must have a mindset that says "I'm not going to give up." I believe many of us have reached a place in our lives where there is a desire to grow. There is a desire to take our businesses to another level. One key factor you must have to operate a business is to be committed. In order to be successful, you must be committed—committed to change, committed to growing yourself, and committed to growing your business. If you feel discouraged or if you feel like you are failing: STOP. Adjust your feelings.

Have confidence in yourself. Read Philippians 1:6 "Being confident of this very thing that he which hath begun a good work in you, will perform it until the day of Jesus Christ". Things will come in your life to try to get you off focus, but don't lose your passion. Be determined. Do not give up. Show up 100% because God sees your effort.

Stay Focused

You will encounter new things each and every day. It is important to remain focused. You have to do more than just show up; you have to put in the necessary work to see your dreams come to reality. You must always apply this kind of dedication to your business. An entrepreneur works all day, every day, working on solutions to improve their business.

Dedication and Sacrifice

There is a personal sacrifice to be taken in order for your business to grow. Why? Because when you believe in yourself and you believe in your dreams, you have to work hard to achieve them. But the hard work pays off in the end. For me, being a single parent came with a sacrifice. Partying had to cease, dating was on hold, and I knew financially things had to change. I quickly learned that you can't achieve anything without letting some things go. In order to be successful, you must sacrifice your time. You must be unselfish with yourself and your time. Working hard will require you to work late hours to meet deadlines and to make sure the budget is met. It will require you to go out of your way to see that your business is a success. While in the growing stages, you might never hear thank you or receive recognition, but that shouldn't stop you from dedicating yourself and putting a plan in motion. Wherever it is that you see your business going, it should encourage you enough to take the necessary steps to make it happen.

Recognize that competition is all around. There is someone competing for a position on the basketball court. Someone is competing for love. Someone is competing for attention. There is competition at your job. How will you deal with this competition? Will you fold or make the decision to become a team player? Have a determined mind that you are a WINNER. I remember when I chose to take on the role of becoming a personal assistant to the bishop of my church. I didn't understand what the position involved. Over time, I realized that being successful involved two things: patience and service. How do you serve through your own struggles? As a single parent, I had to hold down a full-time job. That was not an easy task, but I worked hard, and the hard work, commitment, and sacrifice paid off.

In my comings and goings, I've learned that truly successful people want to see other people succeed. They want to see other people grow. Place a

#1 on growing yourself and your business. Be enthusiastic about network marketing. Tap into people: People are important. The #1 represents primary, it is important and must be first on your agenda. Any great leader has to have that ability to serve. Serve others, and serve through your struggles. Your business is a service. While serving your customers, remember that your growth is riding on your ability to succeed. Your business should be a business of service. How can you help others? What does your business have to offer?

At the end of the day, I've also learned that networking is a gift that has been given to business owners. It is a tool used to help expand your business. Networking is a key ingredient. It will cause your business to grow, especially if you follow my simple little rules as they have helped me to grow my side hustle.

Rule#1: Book one networking event per month.

Rule #2: Ask family/friends to host a networking event for you.

Rule #3: Host a ladies night out event once a month—a sure way to include it in your calendar is to book for the next three to six months. Depending on your circle of friends or people you know, your business will take off.

Rule #4: Become involved in community events, such as a mentoring program.

Rule #5: Have an attitude of gratitude for your business and customers will take you a long way. In the end customer satisfaction is your objective. Practice loyalty to your customers and to the community you serve. Invest your time and energy into making your business a success. Successful people make connections with their customers.

Rule #6: Don't forget to follow-up within 24 hours. Making the connection with people ensures that they don't forget who you are or the company you represent.

Just by being committed to these simple rules and putting them into action, you will begin to see your dreams become a reality.

KRISTI BALLARD

Kristi's mission is to help others get online quickly and to DOMINATE their market, whatever market it may be. She is very eager to work with you and take your business to new heights. She will get you on page one of Google GUARANTEED! Recognized as one of 2011's "One of America's Premier Experts," she was a featured guest on "The Ron LeGrand Show" broadcast on affiliates of CBS, NBC, ABC, and FOX across the country.

The best way to contact Kristi is to visit her website KristiBallard.com, email her from the Contact form (Kristi@KristiBallard.com), or call her directly at 321-305-3636.

Facebook Business Page:
http://www.facebook.com/KBallardOnline

Personal Facebook Page:
http://www.facebook.com/ballardkristi

Twitter: @KBallardOnline

LinkedIn: www.linkedin.com/in/kristiballard/

Pinterest: http://pinterest.com/kballardonline/

Instagram: KBallardOnline

YouTube: MyKBallardOnline

CHAPTER 25

NETWORKING IN THE SOCIAL MEDIA AGE – IT'S NOT ABOUT YOU!

by Kristi Ballard

Happiness isn't about getting what
you want all the time, it's about deeply
loving what you already have.
–Kristi Ballard

In a world filled with Twitter, Facebook, LinkedIn, Reality Television, Tablets, iPhones and thousands of gidgets and gadgets there are enough distractions in life today where people can easily lose sight of real world connections and social interactions. With all the recent developments in technology, society as a whole has become more detached from the personal touch. As time goes by and more technological advancements are made it will be ever more important to make personal connections. For those that can master networking and building relationships in today's digital and social media age, the world will be at their fingertips and happiness as well as opportunities will abound. For those that can't master social media there are always those you can hire for your social media management!

Networking today is truly an art form. Not only must you be technologically savvy but also have the ability to bring that connection into the real world and build relationships. With the proper skill set, focus and personality, connections can be made easier than ever thanks to the social media age, but they can also be broken just as quickly if you aren't careful. When done correctly you will no longer have to go seek out new customers, they will seek you. This is called Inbound Marketing.

Fresh out of College, I landed a position as a flight attendant with a major airline. At a very young age I found myself in an extremely challenging position with the responsibility of taking care of people's lives in extremely unusual circumstances. Along with that responsibility also came more experiences than most people get to have in a lifetime as well as having the freedom of the world at your fingertips. I met so many people in the process and, boy, did I take advantage of that freedom. My passions for learning, travel, adventure and soaking up whatever I can around me have always led me to new experiences, opportunities and connections. Through the freedom to travel came the opportunity to work for a real estate marketing company where I would meet with real estate investment companies nationwide and connect our projects with real estate investors looking for great deals. From the opportunity of working with that marketing company and as a Realtor, grew my fascination and intrigue with the internet and things which today are known as internet marketing (ie. Search engine optimization, social marketing, search engine marketing, etc.). Are we seeing how all our experiences and opportunities connect?

I love to read and seek out things in life that are not ordinary everyday hobbies as for most people. Meeting new people and finding out what they are all about is one of the most intriguing things for me, however it grows harder and harder to make time to make connections with the daily grind and others' busy schedules. Throughout the past 16 years of my life I have lived in 17 different cities in seven different states across the country, therefore Social Media has been an amazing tool for me to keep the connections to my friends and family. It is hands down the number one way I have been able to keep the relationships I've had throughout my life as well as to build new ones and grow my business. Through sharing my life with others and showing love and gratitude for those that I share it with, I have been able to build and maintain a large network where at any given time I can interact with friends, family and colleagues.

When building relationships whether online or in person, it is imperative NOT TO focus on yourself. Yes, you want to share information and put content out there that relates to you in some way but most importantly you want to do one of two things: help other people solve their own problems or entertain them enough to take them away from their own reality for a period of time.

Some of my closest friendships were built from periods of time in my own life when I was going through my biggest struggles and most personal tragedies. Instead of closing myself off and sulking, I chose to face the reality of what was happening and opening up and sharing what I was actually going through. Looking back at it all and evaluating it I was showing to the other person that I was real, that I had real problems and real issues just like everyone else. When you can face the reality of your own life both good and bad as well as search for answers, you never know who may show up with an answer. Back in January of 2011 I was chosen to be interviewed on a Television show with several different industry experts from a variety of fields. While filming the show, I met an amazing woman named CJ who I immediately just clicked with. We began talking about our hobbies and families not ever really discussing why we were there. When filming was over we exchanged numbers and went on our way. Within weeks after meeting we both ended up going through similar major life changes and were able to reach out and help each other forming a bond that we never would've had if we hadn't connected through social networks. Since then we have collaborated on business projects, attended business events, connected each other to more friendships and have a very strong bond. That's the power of social networking at work and if done correctly anyone can do it!

Throughout my studies, personal experiences and work with businesses I've put together my top five ways to networking in today's social media age. Whether you are at a large business event or working with your network online, these top five are surefire ways to build a bond with everyone you meet.

Listen to what people are saying

Don't just dive in empty handed. Before you jump into a conversation and start talking, LISTEN to what people are saying. Nobody likes to be sold to and they definitely don't want to hear all about you. Take some time and see what people are talking about. When you first meet someone don't let the first thing out of your mouth be I'm so and so and this is my company; that's selling. Find out what people are interested in, what are they talking about, if they have a problem they are trying to solve or are looking for someone to help them do something.

Be Yourself

Show some of your personality. Not everybody is the same and we all bring strengths, weaknesses and a variety of hobbies into any type of relationship. What differentiates each one of us is our personality, hobbies and ability to relate to others. What attracts someone to want to get to know you is what you have on the inside that protrudes on the outside. Try to be as transparent as possible and do the things that you love. The more others feel like they really get to know you, the more they are open to share with you and want you to share back with them. When you connect with me online you will be sure to see that I am a Hawaiian Hula Dancer and travel often for fun and to surf all over the world.

Be Genuine

Ask questions about what a person likes to do in their free time. Get to know who they are on a personal level. When you speak from the heart and soul with true wonder, others can see it.

Identify

Look for something that you have in common or areas where you can either personally help them or can connect them to someone who you know for sure can.

LISTEN!

Did I mention first and foremost to listen to what people are saying?

Once you've made a connection with someone in person, take that connection into the social realm and invite them to connect with you online and vice versa. You'll find you may have friends or other hobbies in common and have much more to talk about in the long run. Listen to what they have to say and engage with them then monitor the feedback, further building on what you have started.

Not everyone has the ability to connect with others and keep up relationships in today's busy, distracting world. However when you learn to master the art of networking and have the ability to make those connections last you will find that today's social media age when done correctly can deepen the bonds that you already have. Loving those bonds and nurturing them will bring you happiness, fulfillment and business no matter what industry you are in.

CATHLEEN WILLIAMS
RN, ESQ., LLM

Minister, attorney, registered nurse, author, and media personality—Cathleen is a woman of compassion, authenticity, and commitment. She is an inspirational speaker with a unique message of triumph and hope derived from her life experiences. Cathleen is the regional chair of New York State International Men's Day and the author of *Single Mother the New Father*, a book series for single mothers. Volume 1 Sports is available now; Volume II Raising the Village is expected in 2014.

CHAPTER 26
NETWORKING FOR YOUR CHILDREN

By Cathleen Williams, RN, Esq., LLM

But if any provide not for his own, and specially
for those of his own house, he hath denied the
faith, and is worse than an infidel.
−1 Timothy 5:8

It is common knowledge that entrepreneurs should employ the skill of networking in order to achieve outrageous success in their businesses. While I always felt I had much to improve upon when it came to networking for my business, as a mom I was the woman who was out everywhere, talking to everyone to find out how to prepare my child for the most outrageous success in life. Innately I knew, beyond a shadow of a doubt, that if my son were to have an advantage in this world, he would have to have a great deal of support and even more contacts. It seemed like a no brainer to me because, when I was in school—whether it was nursing school, law school, or when I went back for my master's degree in health law—daily I came across students and professors who had people in their lives providing them with contacts and connections. Rarely did I encounter students trying to figure out life on their own. Most of my classmates had someone in the background making things happen for them.

As a young teenager, I can recall auditioning for admission to the Fiorello LaGuardia High School of Music and Art in New York City. I was a cellist and a pianist, I loved music, and I was a decent musician. Like the hundreds of other students auditioning for Music and Art, I had been playing music for several years. When the time came for me to prepare for my audition, I assumed it was simple. GO in and play. I was totally unaware of the process happening around me with my parents and others who were doing their best to position me for success. My sister was a student there, so she filled me in on the faculty and how the process would go. A neighbor and a dear friend was on the faculty there and she also gave me tips on how to prepare for audition day. She told me where I should go, to make sure to bring snacks, how long would I be there, who I should speak to; simple things that made all the difference on that day. I remember being calm and feeling totally prepared on the morning of my audition. Well rested and well fed. I looked around at the other prospective students. Many of them were uncomfortable, disheveled, looked stunned, like a deer staring into the headlights. As I look back on that day, these students had no preparation or guidance about the audition process. They had no-one fending for them or "networking" on their behalf. Without guides, they had no-one to make sure their experience was not more complicated by basic things like being hungry.

I also remember that our neighbor, the teacher, stopped by the audition room to check on me and wish me good luck. That was a wonderful feeling. I am sure I performed so much better because I felt comfortable, nourished, and prepared for the long wait in the audition room. And I was one of a small percentage of students who actually got accepted into the school that year.

I will never forget that experience. It was my orientation into parents networking for their children: My parents did it for me, I was the beneficiary of their networking, although no-one called it networking; at that time it was better known as "the village.". Whatever the name, it was parents and a community doing everything possible (and legal) to give children an advantage and a great start in life. Given the economy, fast pace, and how competitive the world is today, it is essential that parents have a formal plan for networking on behalf of their children. Whether it is to get them a job, get them into a great school, or find them the best extracurricular activities around, a parent taking the initiative to build a network for their children— and I mean from a young age—can and will make a huge difference in their children's lives.

As a single mother, it was pretty much up to me to network and get support for my son, but also support for myself as his mom. It was impossible to be everywhere and do everything for my child. It is hard for two parents to coordinate chauffeuring children around. My son is an athlete, and if your children are into sports (if they are not, they should consider it), you know that playing children's sports is a huge time and energy commitment - for the children and the parents. For me it was like having a second full-time job.

Every morning it was something. "Mom, I need new sneakers,""Mom, I have a tournament?"—"Mom, I have a game/practice, can you take me? Mom, the coach says I need more practice. Mom, _____(fill in the blank)." Some things I was able to do, but others I couldn't and I quickly learned I did not have to do! By networking with other parents, I could share lots of the responsibility for transporting my child everywhere for everything. Carpooling may not sound like networking but it is! You would be amazed at what you can learn just driving across town to a tournament. Who knew that there were sneakers and sports equipment available free for kids who played in certain summer camps? Who knew that most young kids who loved tennis got jobs at the U.S. Open every summer --and those who did work there got to meet all the great tennis players and learn great job skills while making money doing something they absolutely loved? Who knew? Someone did, and finding out who was networking at its finest on behalf of my son. I made it my job to find out about the many amazing opportunities he was eligible for, and I did it by applying the art of networking for children to raise my son.

Children are unable to navigate this world on their own. They have enough on their little plates. So much to do. If they are active athletes, musicians, or just fun-loving kids, they need help to see and understand things that they would have no clue about but for you, their parent, showing them the way. Not that your children do not have a say in what they do or where they go for help, but likely they will do nothing and go nowhere if they are not gently guided by your loving hand and the hands of your contacts!

When networking for your children, remember that is also a great opportunity to do some networking for yourself. The more expansive *your* network, the better you are able to provide your children with the resources and information they need to accomplish the goals they have for their lives. Of course, you have goals too, and the same people that are helping your children will help you!

Who you are is who your children are becoming. They watch you, they see the benefits of your efforts, and they learn from what you do. If you network efficiently and effectively, so will they. If you follow up and thank the people that help you and them, so will they. You seek out a wonderful but seemingly impossible opportunity and watch it come to fruition by the grace of God and the help of your network and so will they.

It is wonderful for children to understand the value of networking, respect it, and do it for themselves. As young adults, whether in high school, away in college, in sports, on the job or throughout their lives, networking will make life easier for your children. If you are reading this book, you already understand the value of networking, so no need for me to beat that drum again. What I would like to do instead is share with you some of the successes my son Sean and I had as a result of using our networks to increase our net worth.

Sean is a very good tennis player and has been involved in tennis since he could walk. Every program he was in for tennis I found by networking with other parents and through my friends or his grandfather's tennis buddies. One of the tennis programs had an opportunity for a select group of the children from the program to attend Wimbledon's Tennis Tournament in England. While there, the youth athletes competed in the Two Nations Challenge against youth athletes from Andre Agassi's tennis program in Las Vegas. Because I was always present at practices and talking with the coaches, etc., and because Sean was a great athlete, he was one of the few students invited to be a part of the team they took to London. He met Venus Williams, Andy Roddick, and many other professional tennis players who were competing at Wimbledon that year, and it was a life-changing experience for Sean as a 12-year-old athlete.

One of my co-workers at one of my former jobs was married to a high school teacher in charge of the international exchange program at their school. When she shared with me all about this great exchange program and that her husband was taking students to Barcelona, I asked if it was possible for Sean to be included in that year's group. She checked it out; they made an exception for Sean to attend and *voila!* He spent an incredible winter in Barcelona.

Not long after Sean graduated from college, his former coach referred him for a job as a graduate student fellow assisting the women's tennis team at a prestigious university. Through more networking, Sean got the position and a full scholarship to pursue his Masters in Business Administration. He now holds an MBA in Marketing that was paid for by a fellowship he got through our networking.

It used to be my story that networking was not my thing. I would tell people I wasn't good at it and that I really disliked networking. Once I saw what I was able to accomplish for my son, I had to admit that networking was my forte and I was brilliant at it. Now, thank God, I am an amazing networker for myself.

Here are a few important tips when networking for your children:

1. Have a plan and know what you want to accomplish. You can always change later, but avoid going in blind so you are putting your children's lives in someone else's hands.

2. Do your research. Know what is available to you and what you might need to reach the people who can support you.

3. Be safe. Everyone who offers to help you with your children does not have your children's best interests at heart. Never leave your children with someone you do not know or allow anyone to convince you to involve your children in something that sounds suspect. Follow your gut, stay with your children, and teach them how to use their own discernment.

According to Harvard Business School, 65% to 85% of all jobs are found through networking. As networking produces jobs, it can also produce incredible opportunities for children, like trips to Spain and London and even fellowships leading to advanced degrees.

The next time you have a thought about how to make sure your child becomes all they can be, remember that no child stands alone. A parent's role is to prepare their children for the future by giving them the tools needed to live their best life.

> *Train up a child in the way he should go; and*
> *when he is old he will not depart from it.*
> —Proverbs 22:6

ROGERNELLE GRIFFIN

Rogernelle Griffin is an academic development professional with 17 years of expertise in mentoring, counseling, and retention of special populations in a college setting. A native New Yorker, Rogernelle has served in leadership positions in several civic, social, and professional organizations. She is also a proud member of Delta Sigma Theta Sorority Incorporate and can be reached at rogernelle@yahoo.com

CHAPTER 27

EXPANDING YOUR WORLD THROUGH PROFESSIONAL AND SOCIAL ORGANIZATIONS

by Rogernelle Griffin

When I think about my personal networking history and the benefits, I realize that a great deal of my success can be attributed to my memberships in both professional and social organizations. Although these organizations by design provide the opportunity to gain leadership ability and improve presentation skills, the social interaction also allows you to connect to people personally and professionally, to whom you may not otherwise have access. If you are trying to grow your business and expand your base, these organizations are a great way to accomplish those goals.

With journalism as my major in college, I became a student member of the National Association of Black Journalists. This was way before the internet and fingertip access to information, and I found out about the organization through a newsletter. At their national convention that year, I ended up with an internship through their job fair, and subsequently every job I acquired in that field was through networking within that organization. That internship opened the door to a relationship between the newspaper I worked for and the communications program at my college. In addition, I met some of the most prominent figures in print and broadcast news and was mentored by managing editors of newspapers from all over the country. That connection opened a lot of doors for me and others that followed, I'm sure, because I was the only person of color and sometimes the only female at every newspaper outlet that I worked for.

After I left the field of journalism, I became a social worker for the City of New York. Two organizations that propelled my professional development at that time were the Association of Black Social Workers and Social Services Employees Union Local 371. Being a part of these two organizations became my foray into leadership—first, by becoming a shop steward for the union and, second, by serving on committees within the professional organization. Whenever there was a conference, seminar, or retreat, I attended. As the saying goes, you have to be in it to win it! And I was.

That period in my life was also my first exposure to a social organization, the Coalition of 100 Black Women. I was invited to join by the aunt of a friend of mine, and it was the first time I had come face to face with polished, professional women of color who weren't connected to my job. Many were married to prominent men and very much successful in their own right, yet the organization was about civic responsibility and philanthropy. I was in my mid-twenties and still growing professionally, and as I look back on that experience, it changed my self-perception in a way I hadn't realized until now. Without even knowing it, I began a quest to become one of those women.

After graduate school, I began a career in higher education. By then, I understood the necessity of professional organizations for professional development and networking. I joined the Association of Equality and Excellence in Education, a regional group of student support program professionals that was part of a larger national body called the Council for Opportunity in Education. In a short time, I was elected to the board of directors and chaired committees as well as organized conferences and training seminars. I quickly rose to the rank of president of that organization and eventually board secretary of the national group. The contact with colleagues all over the country afforded me personal and professional connections that I would have never have acquired if I had only focused on the job and not the larger role I played in the field. Finding and knowing your place in the world allows everything you do to extend way past your doorstep.

Seeking an active interest in my community, I served on the local Community Board for three years. I learned about the issues that affected where I live and was able to hear about and give input on new developments, zoning changes, and community concerns. I also found out just how much and how little the residents of an area are considered when it comes to economic development. Political activism is another great way to make connections and broaden your base—whether it is joining a political action group or a local governing entity.

Although most people associate Greek Letter Organizations with undergraduate college life, I joined a sorority, Delta Sigma Theta Sorority, Incorporated, through an alumnae chapter in my thirties. The connection to my experience as part of the Coalition of 100 Black Women cannot be overlooked when I think about why I sought membership in Delta. I had been young and a little unsure of myself 10 years earlier, but when the opportunity presented itself to join this organization of professional women, I was ready. I had blossomed professionally and had become personally polished, and I knew what and how I wanted to contribute to the world.

And like I said before, while the social aspect of my sorority is apparent, let's be clear: Delta Sigma Theta is far more than just a sorority. It's a sisterhood of professional, educated women committed to public service. As a result of that sisterhood, there is a level of networking that goes beyond the exchange of business cards. There is what can be considered an obligation to see yourself through your sister's eyes, thereby wanting her to achieve her goals with the same fervor you expect for yourself. If it's in your sorority sister's ability to do, consider it done.

This courtesy is also extended throughout the Pan Hellenic Greek letter organizations, and is an added bonus. You don't always get that with professional contacts. Black Greek Letter Organizations were once considered to be the "talented tenth" of the race, and although the racial demographics have changed to become more inclusive, the mission of academic and professional excellence as well as social responsibility for all of these organizations remains the same today.

I recently attended Delta's 51st National Convention celebrating its centennial year. A week of activities highlighted the sorority's 100-year history of social action, public service, philanthropy, and support of the arts with celebrity-studded tributes. What resonated for me, however, was the bond of women of varying ages, cultures, and experiences sharing a love of and commitment to the largest public service organization in the world. Women who are by profession educators, politicians, scientists, social workers, artists and more, were connected to a cause that transcends individuality, yet propelled by it.

Is seeking membership in professional organizations beneficial to building your personal brand and growing your business? Absolutely! The key is having something to bring to the table. If you don't come with a desire to contribute to the good of the group through your own skills, abilities, and resources, there will be no benefit for you or the group. When I was just beginning my professional life, I had very little experience and quite frankly I had no clue who I was or what my goals were. But I signed up to work on committees and rub elbows with people who were where I wanted to be. I brought enthusiasm and the good sense to listen, learn, and shadow others, which helped elevate me to the next level.

DARLENE AIKEN

Darlene Aiken is an internationally published author and founder of the award-winning Inner Beauty Solutions, Inc., and the Miss Black Collegiate USA Scholarship Pageant. She is an adjunct college lecturer, professional speaker, self-esteem expert, and pageant coach. She has dedicated more than two decades to empowering girls and young women. Her work has been seen in local, national, and international publications, including *Essence*, *Newsday*, *Urbanology*, and *Splash*. She has been recognized by the WNBA and others.

CHAPTER 28
WORK THE ROOM!
by Darlene Aiken

I subscribe to the maxim that, if you are the smartest person in the room, find another room. Networking assists entrepreneurs with never having to worry about being the smartest person in the room; rather, the most connected equates to more customers, when done correctly. As you meet new business people, you are constantly being exposed to other brilliant minds and new events that shape, challenge, and nurture fresh ideas. In this chapter, you will learn eight networking steps to maximize your potential.

Step One:

Always be willing to attend events—you need to always "be somewhere." Sitting at home will not help you make contacts, nor will it get your name out there. You need to know people, and they need to know you and your work. When your face becomes familiar in a variety of professional networking events, people will approach you and want to know who you are and what it is that you offer. They become curious about how you are invited to so many places. Even if they are not in attendance, they might see your face in pictures that were taken at the event.

Just before I started my company, Inner Beauty Solutions, I worked part-time for a woman whom I admired. We will call her Roberta for the purposes of this story. Roberta owned her own business; her husband was a teacher, and he too had a side business. They both operated their businesses from their home office, and I worked as her receptionist. Roberta received invitations to attend many high society events and was often asked to sit on boards, facilitate workshops and presentations, serve as the mistress of ceremonies, and more. I was in awe because I knew that was exactly what I wanted to do.

As it turned out, while Roberta was attending all of these functions, she was not tending to her financial business and could no longer afford to pay me, and I could not afford to volunteer. Needless to say, I ended up leaving and found another job.

As I began to spend countless nights on my computer, in bookstores, and in libraries, conducting research about what it takes to become a successful business owner, I joined a variety of organizations that afforded me the opportunities to attend events that I otherwise would not have been privy to. As a result, I met different people and became exposed to a world of information and places. Eventually, while I was attending these events, I would bump into Roberta from time to time. She thought I was attending these events as an assistant to someone who was speaking or in some other manner other than being a "big wheel" at the events in my own right. Finally, one day, she attended an event and was stunned to discover that I was not only in attendance, but I was one of the honorees. This is how far attending events and networking had taken me.

Step Two:

While you are in attendance, always take the opportunity to speak. Do not complain. Do not act like a know-it-all, and do not take up more than the allotted time. However, do ask a question or two and wait for the answer. I am not a proponent of the adage that there are not any stupid questions, so think through what you're going to say, first. You cannot risk looking like someone who is just speaking for the sake of speaking. If you look as if you lack intelligence, then you will lose out on prospective clients. When you are preparing to speak, always project your voice, stand up straight, speak with confidence, and Always! Always! Always! introduce yourself and your company.

Step Three:

Take no more than five like-minded business professionals with you and no fewer than three. Please do not confuse this statement, as I am not referring to your best girlfriends. I want to be explicitly clear that I mean people—whether male or female—whom you trust and who are like-minded business professionals. It is imperative that you discern this step closely. If done in a haphazard manner, it can be to your detriment. However, when acted upon wisely, it can not only benefit you, but also those on your team. Your teammates do not necessarily have to be in business with you or in the same business. Just make certain that they are trustworthy and are serious about conducting ethical business.

Five team members is the maximum and will allow you to become super-efficient; three should be the minimum as it, too, will permit efficiency, albeit obviously not on the same level as five. To take fewer could work, but of course it will mean more work on your part while more than five could prove problematic.

You're probably wondering at this juncture, what I am getting at. No worries, you are about to find out in the next step.

Step Four:

Normally when people attend events with their family and/or friends, they all sit at the same table together and enjoy themselves. Keep in mind that you are attending these events to network. As you all came together, it is obvious that you know one another; therefore, there is no need to sit together or you waste valuable opportunities to meet great folks who can assist in the building of your businesses.

Each of the people you have brought with you should sit at different tables. There is no strategy for selecting a table. Use your manners; do not sit at reserved tables that are not for you or your team, but sit spread out across the venue. Here is what will happen: Not only will you meet new people, but your team will each meet new people who in turn will introduce you all to new people.

Here is where the trust comes in. Each of you is responsible for getting business cards, contact information, etc., but you also have a responsibility to do the following: Let the new people whom you meet know about each person on your team and let them know that you will be sharing their information and that, before the day/night (whichever is applicable) is over, you would like to introduce them to that person. This is necessary; you will see why later.

If you are fascinating enough—and I am certain that you are—they will want to introduce you to a person or two whom they know, and the networking will begin. In the age of Facebook, once you all go back to your home or

office—heck, in the age of technology, before you go back to your car—
you can friend someone on Facebook. Once you do that, you'll be surprised
at how many friends you all have in common already. Let the networking
begin! Please discern wisely. Do not push your business card onto folks and
do not ask for cards from folks who do not seem serious about conducting
business.

Step Five:

Share! Remember when I talked about trust? Here is why. Of those who
came in your group to the event, you MUST be able to trust them and they
MUST be able to trust you! You should all have introduced each other or
made some kind of contact with those whom each of you met and should
have made some type of introduction to the others. Sometimes, depending
on the event, this might not be possible. If it is not, the responsibility is
incumbent upon each of you to make mention of each other. Not only will
this allow you all to further your contacts, but it looks good when you know
others in a variety of professions. This also elevates you and makes you look
as if you're resourceful. You might be just starting your business, but you
still have resources. You might not have as many as someone who has been
in business longer, but sometimes, one is all it takes. Remember, perception
is everything. This does not mean be untruthful, but it simply means that you
need to utilize everything that you have and strive to do better.

Now that you and your team members have begun to share your newly
acquired resources, you will come to see how many different people will
be available to network with you. You might only benefit from one at this
time, but that is one more than you had. That one could have tentacles to two
or three business contacts that are instrumental to your growth. Also, keep
in mind that, just because you're not able to (or think you're not able to)
do business with someone right now, it does not mean that will be the case
within a month or so. It also does not mean that they are not connected with
someone that they might want to refer you to. This is another reason why
you must operate decently and in order.

Step Six:

Introduce yourself to your newfound colleagues and potential business
partners/customers. Send a follow-up email, make a phone call, or engage in

177

some type of correspondence that you agreed to when you met them. If you did not have the opportunity to meet them, make certain that you remind them of the event and the day. Make sure you personalize each one. It does not matter how many people you met; no one wants to receive correspondence that sounds as if it were intended for someone else.

Ask them if you can keep them on your mailing list. If they see something that is beneficial to them and/or someone within the body of their network, ask them to feel free to pass the information on. Be certain not to bombard them to the point that they become nauseated. Also, be cognizant of what you send out. Make sure it is proofread and accurate.

For those whom you really want and need to impress, carry thank you cards with you to networking events. When you receive business cards from those whom you wanted to meet, utilize a portion of the break time to complete the thank you card and seal it. When the networking event is over, drop it into the nearest mailbox so that they will receive it within the week. Now that is impressive!

Step Seven:

Now that they are on your mailing list, get busy inviting them to try your products or services for a discounted price or give a FREE sample. Invite them to upcoming events and make sure there are perks for your special guests, like them. Remember, timing is everything.

Step Eight:

Follow up! If you agreed to call or set up a face-to-face meeting, SCHEDULE IT AND DO! So many times professionals lose out because they fail to follow up.

If you follow these steps, you will be sure to work the room, and networking will pay off for you in more ways than one.

SHANNOYA FELLOWS

Shannoya Fellows is an entrepreneur by way of education and experience. Raised in a family with women who were always large and in charge, it was inevitable that she should live up to the same! With two management degrees, experience, and creativity, she is destined to leave a trail for the women who will follow in her family. Shannoya believes that, just like someone taught her the many aspects of business and marketing, she is supposed to pass on that same bit of knowledge to you!

Websites: http://www.hairbedazzled.com

www.hairstudio1724.com

Email: info@hairbedazzled.com, Shannoya.fellows@gmail.com

FB page: https://www.facebook.com/hairstudio1724

Instagram: @hairbedazzled, @hairstudio1724

CHAPTER 29

MY BACK POCKET TOPIC

by Shannoya Fellows

Most people think that networking is simply showing up at events to pass along cards or using social media and contact information to showcase their business to as many people as they possibly can. If this is your idea of networking, you only understand half the equation! Just because you give someone your name does not mean that they will remember it, even if they are generally good with names. You have to make people remember you and your business. Sounds like you should fill someone's head with information about your business products or services, right? Wrong! The key is to find out what people need and create a desire in them for whatever product or service you offer. Do this by being an excellent listener and conversationalist, taking mental notes, and mastering your back pocket topic.

Now having the attributes that I mentioned above takes time to develop, but you can start developing them today. The reality of business owners today is that people care more about themselves than they care about you. Ever wonder about why Apple was able to dominate the market the way they did? They created a desire through marketing. Companies like Apple have been proven to succeed because they understand the philosophy of egoism, which suggests that humans are by nature self-centered. Even the name iPhone represents this philosophy; the creator of this name is a marketing genius. The next time you are having a conversation, count how many times you hear the words "I," "me," and "my." People enjoy talking about themselves, their stories, their desires, their needs, etc. The best way to persuade is by listening. **You can find out so much about a person by listening, so you need to create a desire in yourself to listen to others to find out exactly what it is that they need.**

It is important as a networking expert to listen—not just listen, but listen attentively. Over the years, I have managed to perfect this skill. I never thought that I would be able to seal my lips and give others the floor; actually it took many years of my life to develop this skill. I was once told by a very wise man that I love hearing myself speak; I still do and it is imperative that I do, but I have since learned to share the microphone. Allowing others to take the mic helped me perfect my listening skills. It also gave me an advantage. I began learning so much about people. Sometimes, through conversation, business ideas would pop into my head. I would sometimes wish I had a product or service to offer just by listening to someone speak.

Talking to people and listening helped me recognize the entrepreneur in me in my earlier years. I remember a time when a young lady expressed to me her struggle to keep her marriage alive. I suggested that she and her husband start to enjoy life and do things the way they used to before they had children, by going on dates, vacations, etc. She indicated that their family was in other places and she didn't really have anyone to babysit the children other than during daytime hours. This need in her sparked an idea in me: to start an overnight care or short-term care (up to a week) service. Now this was a niche because I did not know another child care company like that. I never started this business because I had many other ideas afterwards, but just listening to her story influenced my thinking. If I had a child care business or anything remotely close to that, she could have been my new client and I know there would have been many more like her. I did not know this young lady, but just meeting her had sparked a conversation at a make-up party, proving that you can start a conversation and discover others' needs at any time and at any place!

I am quite the conversationalist, and you should be too. Learn to spark a conversation and once again: listen! Always have a **back pocket topic** as a conversation tool. Be careful not to sound like an infomercial. This topic starter should be a roadway to your business. Use comments or questions that can lead up to the product or service that you offer. Depending on the product or services you offer, you can observe your target and make an assessment of which back pocket topic you will use to start your conversation. You should definitely have more than one. I am a manager at Hairstudio1724 in Brooklyn, NY, an upscale salon and spa, as well as the upcoming owner of the hair product line "Hairbedazzled." My ability to start a conversation and listen has given me a competitive edge in this highly competitive industry. I offer beauty services and products; therefore, my back pocket topic generally revolves around beauty. My target audience is women of all types.

Now, what woman doesn't like a compliment? I am confident enough to tell another woman how beautiful she looks or how much I love her shoes, her hair, nails, etc. This industry allows me to start a conversation with almost any woman in just about any location (grocery store, mall, post office, bank, etc.), so long as the timing is right. The places that I generally go to are filled with women, so I never go home without making a connection. The sidewalk you walk on can be your market place!

One day I was making my routine run to the bank. It was a bright and sunny afternoon, and an older African American woman with lusty long black hair was walking in front of me. She was an older woman, about 50 years old, and her hair hung to about four inches below her shoulders. I looked at her hair and decided to speed up a bit. Her hair was visibly thinning, and I decided to use this as a reason for her to consider my salon. I said hello once I was side by side and followed up with, "You have such beautiful long hair." She thanked me with a big smile. I proceeded with my line: "It's long and healthy, but looks like it should be a lot thicker than it is. Are you using a brushing method to straighten your hair?" She looked surprised and answered "yes" with a how-did-you-know expression. After I introduced myself, she seemed anxious to talk about her hair, so I listened attentively as she told me about the salon that she visits, what they do, and the products they use. She had also noticed her thinning hair, but assumed t it was because of age. When she had told me enough, I began to tell her that my salon has corrected a lot of thinning hair issues that seemed to be an epidemic even in younger women. I gained more of her interest when I told her the master stylist at my salon discovered that thinning hair can also be caused by the brushing method used to straighten hair. I briefly explained to her the techniques and correction treatments that we use. She seemed really impressed and began asking me questions about it. I wrapped it up by handing her my business card and telling her that I looked forward to seeing her soon. A few weeks later, I was told by the manager that she had come in and was very impressed by the environment and the services. She also spoke very highly of me. Two weeks after her visit, I saw her in the salon and we began talking. She thanked me for approaching her by the bank and said that she had noticed a huge difference in her hair already. Once she began developing trust, she also took advantage of our other services: facials, make-up, massages, etc. In a matter of a few weeks, she had her daughter and sister coming to the salon. They each required different hair services. She is now one of our most loyal customers and refers clients all the time. Her cousin found us on our Facebook fan page and sent an email requesting a consultation for her wedding. This summer we provided beauty services to her cousin and entire bridal party for her wedding. She continues to refer friends and family to our salon, and I am proud to say that this Sistah has long thick luscious hair thanks to Hairstudio1724 in New York.

In essence I used my back pocket topic to smooth out the approach and get a smile as well as genuine interest from this woman. Although I led the conversation, I listened to her. I gave her just enough information to capture her interest. This was not just a sales pitch; it was a conversation! Once she walked into the salon, we had the advantage of being able to offer her products and services that fit her needs. We also had the opportunity to grow through her circle with our customer relationship management methods and tools. From the client's first visit, the receptionist captured her contact information as well as her services of choice. I was able to connect with this client on Facebook and gained exposure to her circle of friends and family. Her daughter is a young adult, and we follow her and vice versa on Instagram to network through a younger generation of women. This is the type of networking that I live for. I reached out to this client locally and connected with others in her circle virtually. The next time you are walking to the bank—or anywhere for that matter—look around for your target audience and pull out your **back pocket topic**.

TAYLOR STEPHENS

Taylor is a 15-year-old high school student and the daughter of Toni Coleman-Brown. Taylor attends York Early College Academy in Queens, New York. She is taking both high school courses and college courses at York College. She is popular and well-liked by a large circle of friends. When she graduates from high school, she plans on attending Howard University in Washington, DC.

CHAPTER 30

NETWORKING: LEARNING FROM THE BEST

by Taylor Stephens

Sometimes I think my mom (Toni Coleman-Brown) is crazy. When she asked me to write a 1,500-word essay for her new book, I thought, *OMG! What is this woman thinking?* Then when she spoke to me and explained the value of being a part of this project, I decided to give it a shot.

I think networking is a tool that entrepreneurs use to get clients and customers, but for me and at my age, networking is about making new friends. Growing a network of friends is a big part of growing up. Like my mom, I make new friends everywhere I go. For example, I had to make new friends when I went to my new school and now that I'm going to high school, I'm sure that I am going to make even more friends.

I believe that going to school is similar to networking, but instead of getting new customers, I gain new friends. Having a strong network of friends is important to me. It means that I have people that I can talk to, gossip with, and go shopping and to the movies with. Friendship means being able to have people around that I can depend upon when I need them. They also help me with things like homework, advice, and big challenges. Having friends is a big part of my personal growth. Developing good people skills will help me when I become an adult because it will help me to deal with people and will teach me how to solve problems, which are all necessary skills to have when seeking to become a good businesswoman.

Since I was a very little girl, I can remember watching my mom deliver lots of presentations. At first I used to hate it when my mom had to speak because it meant that she would be away from home. However, when I got a little older, she began to take me to her events. Watching her speak has encouraged me to do something big in life. It felt good meeting all of the different people who my mom had a huge impact on. I realized that my mother was a really special lady because, not only was she a role model to me, but she was also a role model to other people. My mother has inspired so many adults with her words. She is a phenomenal woman, and when I get older, I want to be just like her.

I can remember earlier this year when my little sister Sasha participated in pageant and my mother needed to know where to go to find her a pageant dress. She knew nothing about the pageant world, so she told us that she remembered a lady named Judy Mae Chao who was a part of her network and also the former Miss Chinese America and model. She recalled that Judy also taught young girls how to prepare for pageants and did image consulting. So she asked Judy where to go to find the perfect dress for Sasha. She found the perfect dress, and my sister was placed in the top 10 in the Junior Miss New York pageant. Even my sister is learning about networking as a result of the influence of my mom. She made a new friend at the pageant. Sasha and her new friend Elizabeth have been hanging out and talking on the phone ever since. My mother's network played a big part in Sasha's success, proving that (yet again) networking pays.

There was another time when my mom used her network to enroll me in a Saturday program for girls sponsored by the national sorority Delta Sigma Theta called the Delta GEM program. I remember one day they had a guest speaker. It was a lady by the name of Darlene Aiken. She was also an author who wrote the book *"How To Be A Lady"*. One thing I remembered her saying was to never chew gum while walking in public. She said it was not ladylike. For some reason, that really stuck out to me. But the most interesting part about this story is that years later my mother ran into Ms. Aiken again—at what? That's right: a networking event! And now Ms. Aiken is part of this book.

While my mom still does a lot of live events, my friends and I like to network online. I have a large social media network. My two favorite social networks are Instagram and Facebook. I have 2,209 friends on Facebook and 4,390 followers on Instagram. Instagram is one of my favorite social networks because I can post videos and also see the pictures of all my friends. I find Facebook interesting because I can keep in contact and chat with my family who live in different states. On Facebook, people get to post status updates and share things, and I like that. I've managed to stay in contact with lots of people because of social networks like Facebook—even friends I made when I went to sleep-away camp many years ago. Social networks really help me see what is going on in people's lives, even when I don't see them that often. For instance, I have family who live in New Orleans, and I've been able to keep in contact with them through social media. Also, Facetime and Skype technology not only help me talk to my friends, but they also allow me to see them virtually. My mom also has a large online network. Her Network for Women in Business has almost 15,000 followers, and my mom herself has almost 3,000 friends on Facebook. She also uses technology to build her network. I don't know where technology will take business and social networking in the future, but I know I will be on top of it because I've learned from the best: my mother and the other ladies who participated in this project. The most important lesson that I've learned is to be patient with myself and others. As a young person, I have a tendency to want everything to happen right away. But I've learned from my mom and her network of friends to be patient and not to rush things. Most people are looking for overnight success, but I now know that it's all a process and that we have to respect the journey as well as each other. Like I said before, I've learned from the best, and that's a fact.

CONCLUSION

Well, after reading the chapters of this book and learning from these amazing and wise entrepreneurs and now authors, I'm sure that one thing is absolutely clear: NETWORKING WORKS! And you're right, it does.

Most businesses don't exist in a vacuum. Businesses need people (clients and customers), and networking connects you with the people you need to succeed, grow, and prosper. I founded the Network for Women in Business with a simple mission: to train, connect, and advance women business owners. This book is a physical manifestation of our mission. Our motto is "We EDUCATE to ELEVATE women in business." I know that after reading this book you probably feel as if you've been taught some valuable lessons, but the learning doesn't have to stop here.

The learning can continue by becoming a part of our tribe. Becoming a member of the Network for Women in Business could be one of the best decisions you could make for your business. Membership connects you with the right people and gives you access to our exclusive Diva Millionaire's Club as well as our amazing training vault, which consists of hours and hours of trainings in the form of teleseminar and webinar recordings that could literally transform your business overnight. In addition, membership gives you access to our exclusive private group coaching program, where you can get all of your most burning business questions answered. We also provide our members with exclusive discounts on all of our products and services.

We have members from all across the world, and our membership base is growing every day. We are quickly becoming one of the hottest networking groups for women on the internet, and with the introduction of our regional directors and the launch of nation-wide chapters, we are quickly becoming one of the most extensive networking groups offline as well.

If you believe that networking can help to increase your net worth, then don't hesitate to become a member of the Network for Women in Business today at http://www.networkforwomeninbusiness.com. You can also call (646-421-0830) or email me (toni@networkforwomeninbusiness.com) if you have any questions.

I am looking forward to connecting with you!

Toni Coleman Brown, Founder
The Network for Women in Business
www.networkforwomeninbusiness.com
www.facebook.com/networkforwomeninbusiness

THE END

CPSIA information can be obtained at www.ICGtesting.com
Printed in the USA
BVOW10s2140091013

333343BV00009B/115/P

9 780957 556119